# FRENCH WATERCOLORS OF THE 20ᵗʰ CENTURY

# FRENCH WATERCOLORS OF THE 20ᵀᴴ CENTURY

by François Daulte

Foreword by André Dunoyer de Segonzac

A Studio Book

THE VIKING PRESS · NEW YORK

Translated from the French by Diana Imber

*Droits de reproduction artistique réservés SPADEM, Paris ;
COSMOPRESS, Genève ; ADAGP, Paris*

© 1968 Office du Livre SA, Fribourg

Published in U.S.A. by The Viking Press, Inc.
625 Madison Avenue, New York, N.Y. 10022

Published in Canada by
The Macmillan Company of Canada Limited

Library of Congress catalog card number : 68-18114

Printed and bound in Switzerland

# CONTENTS

# LIST OF ARTISTS

# FOREWORD BY ANDRÉ DUNOYER DE SEGONZAC

Certain conventions concerning the nature of watercolor seem well established: it is commonly argued, for instance, that an aquarelle must be handled lightly and that transparency ensures perfect freshness of color.

I confess that I do not entirely share this view, for in my opinion watercolor is closely related to oil painting. The ingredients of the colors are the same; the only difference lies in the medium which binds them—gum arabic or linseed oil. Either may be converted into a liquid by the addition of water, oil, or spirits of turpentine. Veronese and Rubens both produced oil sketches with all the fluidity and translucency of watercolor.

Watercolor is not necessarily limited to a simple color scale as an adjunct to a drawing—for example, the Moroccan sketchbooks of Delacroix, Jongkind's aquarelles, beautiful and expressive with a minimum palette; or for instance the Turners, full of color and contrast, and the

watercolors by Signac and Cross, pure color divided and isolated by white in the Neo-Impressionist aesthetic. One might call it watercolor by juxtaposition.

Another approach to watercolor painting is less analytical, more synthetic—as for example the work of Constable, Géricault, Daumier, and Rouault, all of whom, while not insensitive to color and light, sought after sculptural quality and density rather than transparence and brilliance of tone. Color here is superimposed, not juxtaposed.

One day Raoul Dufy said to me:

"How long do you take to do a watercolor?"

"Ten to twelve hours."

"I never take more than two hours," he replied.

It is true that his own work, the product of a magnificent, free, and luminous style, would have lost its spontaneity if worked over. But if we examine the Cézannes of the last period, we realize the degree to which oil and watercolor had become, for the Master of Aix, two very close, almost identical, means of expression. There is the same scrupulous care and economy in the use of white, and the same refusal to accept anything without long observation and meditation. His last works, those painted after the Mont Sainte-Victoire d'Aix-en-Provence, are important in this respect. Whether on paper or canvas, the technique and conception are the same.

André Dunoyer de Segonzac

1 ANDRÉ DUNOYER DE SEGONZAC: *Les Delphiniums* or *Larkspur* (1960). Watercolor, 21 ¼ × 29 ⅞ in. *In the collection of Mr. and Mrs. Josef Rosensaft, New York.*

7

# INTRODUCTION

The American novelist Henry Miller discusses in a recent essay his discovery of a gift for painting and offers a perceptive analysis of the art of watercolor: "Watercolor has affinities with the sonnet or *haiku*, rather than with the lament. It grasps the essential rhythm, the bouquet, the perfume, not the substance. Above all it portrays environment." [1]

*Twentieth-Century Watercolor*

In this volume some of the finest watercolors of the last sixty years are reproduced in an attempt to discern the constant features of this most difficult technique and to follow its evolution from the end of Impressionism to our own times. Encompassing Paul Cézanne and Michel Ciry, Pierre Bonnard, Marc Chagall, and Raymond Legueult; touching on the Nabis, Pointillists, Fauves, and Cubists; the painters of Montmartre and Montparnasse, the Poetic Realists and the New Forces, I have tried to show major paintings by most of the masters since 1900 who have displayed a bias toward the art of watercolor.

Although it is necessary to group the artists and their work largely in historical perspective and to arrange the watercolors by schools and styles, I have nevertheless tried to avoid too rigid a classification. In fact, it is difficult to classify watercolor painters by the usual rules of the history of art, not only because the greater number of twentieth-century artists have disdained wash and gouache, but also because the technique of watercolor evades dogmatic orderliness. In the words of Pierre Cabanne: "[Watercolor] ignores ambition and displays no envy; its modesty is the price of liberty." [2]

1. *Peindre C'est Aimer à Nouveau*, Paris, 1962, p. 50.

2. "L'Ecole Buissonnière de la Peinture," *Arts*, No. 863, 10 April, 1962.

9

Watercolor masters are not necessarily masters of drawing, and conversely. However, several artists, such as Albert Marquet, Raoul Dufy, and André Dunoyer de Segonzac, or more recently Legueult and Ciry, have worked in both mediums with equal success. But other creative artists are not in the least attracted by watercolor painting and refuse to include the slightest application of color into their drawings. Georges Seurat, for instance, never used watercolor. He was an incomparable draftsman, and a Conté crayon was all he required to express himself in shades of black and white, suggesting form and atmosphere with the lightest of touches. On the other hand, Paul Signac and Henri-Edmond Cross, both friends of the founder of Neo-Impressionism, discovered increasingly that watercolor suited their intimate style and enabled them to develop their *tachiste* vision, subject as it was to the slightest changes of light and sky.

The watercolors of Henri Matisse and Pablo Picasso rarely equal their drawings, whereas the watercolors, heightened often with gouache, of Georges Rouault, Marc Chagall, and Maurice Utrillo are far better than their drawings, which are few and relatively unimportant. Such examples are frequent. Suffice it to say that ink or black or red pencil gives some artists the same facility that a wet brush and color wash give to others.

Although several of the painters represented here used watercolor or gouache throughout their careers, others, particularly Cézanne, Bonnard, and more recently Roland Oudot, did not begin to use these techniques until late in life, and sometimes then only by a lucky chance. For instance, in 1930 Bonnard was forced to go to a hospital for treatment. His friend Dr. Hans R. Hahnloser heard him complaining of his forced inactivity and suggested that he should turn his attention to watercolor, which he had neglected since he was a young man, and brought him a paintbox and brushes. "Bonnard," writes Mme. Hahnloser, "set to work. But what was his disappointment! The result was nothing but a kind of brownish gravy—in Spitteler's words, 'if you mix everything up you get only gray.' Bonnard, accustomed by oil painting to retouching and correcting mistakes, explained in a muddled fashion that he had no talent for instant success."[3]

Fortunately Dr. Hahnloser thought of bringing the invalid some gouache, which enabled him to correct his first draft. This produced several technically individual works, in which Bonnard often mixed and heightened his watercolor with white gouache.

The uses of watercolor are of great interest, and it is scarcely necessary to remark that an artist's

3. *Bonnard*, Neuchâtel, 1965, pp. 183-184.

2  ALBERT MARQUET: *The Letter* (1912). Brush and ink wash, 12 ¼ × 9 in. *Private Collection, Paris.*

preference for this method—fundamentally only a means of expression—serves to reveal his deepest nature. It cannot be by chance that Signac, Cross, Marquet, and Dufy barely cover their paper but scatter spots of color side by side. Their working technique thus reveals a link between these four masters, who in other respects are so different. It is also relevant that Rouault's, Maurice de Vlaminck's, and Roland Oudot's addition of gouache to their aquarelles was not a search for immediate and fugitive effects, but an attempt to give solidity and permanence to their subjects.

## A Swift and Inventive Process

I would like to preface my description of the paintings reproduced in this book by discussing watercolors in general, and the different means of using them. The actual materials and the different processes will be more fully discussed in the last section of this work.

With a sheet of paper, a pencil, and a small paintbox the artist can reproduce whatever aspect of the world he wants. Swift and productive, the technique of watercolor is as effective for the realization of an interior vision as for the most fugitive landscape impression, which could never be recorded by the slower methods of oil painting. Paul Signac, in his memorable essay on Jongkind, observes that painting in watercolor

satisfies certain artistic ambitions which work in the studio cannot fullfil.

"A cloudy sky," Signac writes, "is a magnificent composition, but it changes continuously. If you cannot catch it at once, its beauty vanishes and only separate elements of an ephemeral construction are recorded—the stones instead of the cathedral. . . .

"A quick pencil sketch and a few touches of watercolor suffice to fix the composition, movement, and tonal values of the whole, whereas the artist in oils, unless he is a genius, will be caught in his palette and reduced to painting shapeless, jostling splodges of white or gray . . . . The watercolorist, working quickly, runs no risk of introducing contradictory, false, and harmful elements into his composition and he can avoid nature's traps—the infinite succession of possible solutions to a proposition which has only one true answer. Speed of execution and limitation of size will also prevent the artist from adding unnecessary and laborious detail that would deaden his vision.

"Nature is entirely against the oil painter: both the barometer and thermometer make league against him; cold drives him home, the wind blows his easel over, while dust and rain take it in turns to spoil his palette; the tide goes out, and where a few moments ago there was a pretty little boat dancing on the water, now, half an hour later, he is left with a pathetic hulk resting on a sea of mud. But the watercolorist misses nothing, recording everything which brings life

3 YVES BRAYER: *Italian Officer* (1933).
Ink wash, 18 ⅛ × 12 ⅝ in. *Private Collection,
Paris.*

and interest to the main motif. The simplicity of his tools allows him to overcome the elements and even in the worst conditions to catch the most fleeting effect." [4]

*Juxtaposition as a Watercolor Technique*

This technique, simple in appearance only, has been widely used by twentieth-century watercolorists. Such painters as Cézanne, Henri Manguin, Signac, Dufy, or Yves Brayer separate and clearly define their colors by using the white of the paper, and for these artists this manner of handling white *en réserve* forms one of the essential conditions, if not the key to watercolor. They can skillfully suggest an impression of the spectacle that took their eye without covering the paper. "Can there be richer skies or more solid earth than Cézanne's magnificent sketches barely covering a miserable piece of paper, with twenty strokes of watercolor—twenty certainties, twenty victories—but at the cost of what will power?" [5]

The pure watercolorists seek transparency, freshness, and a luminous limpidity rarely afforded by oil color. Like René Char or Philippe Jaccottet, for instance, poets of our time whose language is stripped bare, some artists purposely use only the slightest tones of wash and sepia. "For them," writes Dufy in an unpublished

notebook, "watercolor, which allows the greatest freedom, is scarcely a medium in the material sense. Its speed arises partly from the fact that passages between the colors are themselves formed by the white of the paper. It is a pleasant way of making rapid notes outside and is also useful for working out the color construction of a composition. More should not be demanded. It is the art of intention above all."

Of course watercolor technique requires decision and rapid execution since the colors dry very quickly. Consequently the artist can rarely correct his initial work if he is not satisfied with it. Repentance is futile. Molière wrote a poem called "The Glory of the Val de Grâce," commenting on the work of Pierre Mignard, in which he exactly described the work of the fresco painter, who has to finish his design immediately without retouching, as the color will only adhere to fresh mortar. Molière's rules for mural painting apply equally to watercolor.

[Water-color]
*is hasty and unmercifully demands*
*that the painter adapt himself to her impatient ways ;*
*He must do as she bids and fall bravely to work,*
*Grasping the instant she presents to his hand.*
*The stern severity of this fleeting moment*
*Has no mercy on errors of the brush,*
*In this art there is no point of return ;*
*All must be accomplished on the instant.*

4. P. Signac, *Jongkind*, Paris, 1927, pp. 111-112.
5. *Ibid.*, p. 109.

4 ANDRÉ DERAIN: *The Field* (1903-1904). Brush and ink wash, 11 ⅞ × 18 ⅓ in. *In the collection of Alex Maguy, Paris.*

## Superimposition as a Watercolor Technique

It would, however, be wrong to assume that all artists regard watercolor as work of an instant and immediate nature, which must retain an appearance of spontaneity, and which cannot be worked over. Certain outstanding artists—Dunoyer de Segonzac, Georges Rouault, Chagall, Maurice Utrillo, or Ciry, for instance—still look upon watercolor as a picture, a painting done with water, and because watercolors dry quickly these masters can lay on their corrections almost immediately. They add a form of glaze—in other words, successive and transparent colors. Sometimes they add gouache to their watercolor to give mystery and depth to their work, producing a quality reminiscent of fresco. Hence their watercolor gains in density and brilliance what it loses in transparence. Segonzac's work, nearer to John Constable than to J. M. W. Turner, is important in this respect. This artist would readily agree to a comparison of the successive stages of a watercolor with the different states of a print. Segonzac first makes a rapid charcoal sketch of his chosen subject. Then—the second state—he strengthens the forms of his composition by an ink drawing, by which he accentuates his first ideas and states them more precisely. In the third state he establishes the principal values of his landscape or still life with broad colored areas, and, although the charcoal sketch disappears completely beneath the wash, the ink drawing shows clearly through the watercolors and serves to contain them. In a sense it is the framework of the whole construction. And in the last stage Segonzac places new colors to reinforce the first wash. He modifies his reds, making them more opaque, and heightens the ochers and emerald-greens. "The paper gradually begins to fill. Soon it will be completely covered.... Thus the watercolor achieves unity, weight and resonance at a speed impossible in oil colors." [6]

## An Enhancement of Life

Whereas Segonzac, Chagall, and Roland Oudot prefer to paint on large sheets of paper which enable them to treat their watercolor as a work in its own right, Signac, Cross, and Maurice Brianchon use small portable sketchbooks just for recording the essential features of a landscape that they want to remember, rather than for expressing profound reflections. But twentieth-century watercolors are nearly all spontaneous works, whether they are to be used as a sketch for a larger painting or to remain as they are. Painted in a day, or perhaps even half an hour, they record the immediate, the flashing reaction of an artist to his vision of the external world. Modern masters reveal their originality and freshness of vision in watercolor and gouache more frequently than in their oil paintings. For example, Matisse's smallest watercolor sketches

6. C. Roger-Marx, *Dunoyer de Segonzac*, Geneva, 1951, p. 49.

16

5  ALBERT MARQUET: *Profile of a Seated Nude* (1912). Brush and ink wash, 6¼ × 10⅝ in. *Private Collection, Paris.*

of the dance express the flight of the ballerinas and their airy poses far better than do his great murals at the Barnes Foundation. Likewise the fleeting line of a tree barely hinted at by Cross on an odd corner of graph paper seems to explain the mystery of creation more clearly than his large paintings of Le Lavandou or Saint-Tropez. This is the reason collectors study so closely the water-colors of Cézanne, Edouard Vuillard, or André Planson, in which intentional primitiveness heightens the sense of life. "Some beautiful things," wrote La Rochefoucauld, "are more brilliant in the unfinished state then when perfectly finished."

## Diversity in Twentieth-Century Watercolor

The most striking aspect of the watercolors reproduced here is their diversity. During the last sixty years France, that land of individuals, has apparently found a means of expression as vivid as those of earlier centuries. No particular theory predominates. Every artist looks squarely in the face of reality and tries, as far as possible, to develop the original gifts that have been granted him.

Watercolor frees the artist from those conventions often implied by a picture in oils. When a painter executes a large composition he knows that the public will see and judge his finished work, and this preoccupation with public opinion sometimes forces him into regrettable concessions to fashion. But in a watercolor, often no more than a rough sketch, the tentative outline of an idea, the artist is limited only by his own genius. Accepted ideas do not concern him at all. This accounts for the immediate brilliance of some of Toulouse-Lautrec's or Pascin's washes.

Henry Miller, in the title of the essay quoted earlier, described watercolor painting "as falling in love anew," looking with fresh eyes on the sights and scenes so prodigally offered by the world. Moreover, this love is not possessive, since the artist shares his vision through his work. He helps us to admire things of which we know nothing, and those subjects to which long use has closed our minds. He lends us his eyes to look at the world.

6 EDOUARD VUILLARD: *The Table* (about 1896). Ink wash, 7⅞ × 12¼ in. *Private Collection, Paris.*

# THE ARTISTS

PAUL CÉZANNE

7  *The Boy in the Red Waistcoat* (1890-1895)

Although Cézanne never considered a drawing to be an end in itself—the black pencil and chalk sketches were only preliminary studies for his paintings—after 1888 he turned enthusiastically to the study of watercolor. Even when copying the *Medea* of Delacroix, or Caravaggio's *Entombment*, or painting the countryside near Aix-en-Provence, Mont Sainte-Victoire or the Bibemus quarry, he always tried to resolve the problems of space and light.

Between 1890 and 1895 Cézanne painted four portraits in oils of a young Italian, known by the striking name of Michelangelo di Rosa, who was working in the countryside near Aix. The most famous of these—justifiably, because of its perfection—is the one in the Bührle Collection in Zurich. The rest are all in the United States; one in the David Rockefeller Collection in New York, another in Paul Mellon's collection at Upperville, Virginia, and the third in the Barnes Foundation at Merion, Pennsylvania, near Philadelphia. Cézanne also painted two watercolor portraits of the same model, and the composition of the one shown here is very close to that of the Barnes painting. In both the young boy is portrayed full face, standing out from a lightly sketched background. The oil painting, however, is only a half-length, whereas the watercolor shows the subject almost full-length, seated on a rush-bottomed chair. Perhaps even more than in the oil, the perfection of tone in the watercolor—ash-grays, limpid greens, and vivid reds—evokes the melancholy and pensive dignity of Cézanne's young Italian model.

Watercolor, 18 ⅛ × 12 in.
Unsigned.

*Provenance:* Ambroise Vollard, Paris; Pierre Loeb, Paris; Albert Meyer, Paris; Erich Maria Remarque, New York.

*Publications:* A. Vollard, *Paul Cézanne*, Paris, 1914, reprod., p. 163; I. Arishima, "Cézanne," *Ars*, 14th year, 1926, Pl. 24; L. Venturi, *Cézanne, Son Art et Son Œuvre*, Paris, 1936, Vol. I, No. 1094, and reprod., Vol. II, Pl. 316; G. Schmidt, *Cézanne*, Paris, 1953, Pl. 31; Th. Rousseau, *Cézanne*, Paris, 1953, Pl. 30; Neumeyer, *Cézanne Drawings*, New York, No. 45, with reprod.

*Exhibitions:* A Loan Exhibition of Cézanne, Wildenstein Gallery, New York, 1947, No. 78; Cézanne, The Art Institute of Chicago and the Metropolitan Museum of Art, New York, 1952, No. 74, reprod.; Europäische Meister 1790-1910, Kunstmuseum, Winterthur, 1955, No. 222; Cézanne, Municipal Museum, The Hague, 1956, No. 78, reprod.; Exhibition Commemorating the Fiftieth Anniversary of the Death of Cézanne, Pavillon Vendôme, Aix-en-Provence, 1956, No. 74; Cézanne, Kunsthaus, Zurich, 1956, No. 110, reprod.; Cézanne, Haus der Kunst, Munich, 1956, No. 85, reprod.; Cézanne, Wallraf-Richartz-Museum, Cologne, 1956–57, No. 38; De Géricault à Matisse, Musée du Petit-Palais, Paris, 1959, No. 147, Pl. 31; Cézanne, Oberes Belvedere, Vienna, 1961, No. 39; Cézanne, Gauguin, Van Gogh, Seurat, Kunstverein, Hamburg, 1963, No. 17, Pl. 59; Cézanne Watercolors, Knoedler Gallery, New York, 1963, No. 33, Pl. XXXI; Chefs-d'Œuvre des Collections Suisses, de Manet à Picasso, Palais de Beaulieu, Lausanne, 1964, No. 96, reprod.

*In the collection of Mme. Walter Feilchenfeldt, Zurich.*

23

# PAUL CÉZANNE

8  *Still Life with a Blue Jug* (1904-1906)

This painting, for a long time in the collection of Henri Manguin, is one of Cézanne's last watercolors. We are confronted once again in this work with all the objects that the artist never tired of painting in his later years : apples, a knife, onions, a blue earthenware jug, and a half-empty bottle of wine. It will be seen to what point Cézanne, now at the very end of his career, had mastered the art of handling white; how every brushstroke is the outcome of long observation and thought. A few colors, lightly diluted with water, suffice to place the objects and fruit against their background. The solidity of the knife is suggested, to be sure, by its oblique position on the table but also by the colors. Cézanne, in a letter written on April 15, 1904, to his young admirer Emile Bernard, explained how he saw the problem of space : "Perpendicular lines leading to the horizon give depth. Now nature appears to us in depth rather than space, hence it is essential to introduce into the shafts of light, seen as reds and yellows, enough blue tones to give an airy impression."

It will also be observed how skillfully Cézanne heightened the pencil framework of his still life with touches of watercolor. "Drawing and color," declared the Master of Aix, "are not separate; as you paint you draw; and the better the color harmonies, the more exact the drawing. When color is at its height, form is at its most solid. Contrasts and relationship of tone are the secret of drawing and dimensional form." (Quoted in E. Bernard, *Souvenirs sur Paul Cézanne*, Paris, 1920, p. 39.)

Watercolor, 18 × 22 in.
Unsigned.

*Provenance:* Henri Manguin, Paris; Mme. Lucile Martinais-Manguin, Paris.

*Exhibitions:* Paul Cézanne, An Exhibition of Watercolors, The Arts Council of Great Britain, London, 1946, No. 43; De l'Impressionnisme à Nos Jours, Musée National d'Art Moderne, Paris, 1958, No. 31; De Cézanne à Picasso, Maîtres de l'Aquarelle au xxᵉ Siècle, Musée Jenisch, Vevey, 1962, No. 33, reprod.; Cézanne Watercolors, Knoedler Gallery, New York, 1963, No. 68, Pl. LXIII.

*In the collection of Norton Simon, Los Angeles.*

PIERRE BONNARD

9   *The White Yacht* (Cannes, 1935)

It is as inaccurate to talk of schools and common inspiration for the Nabis as for the Impressionists, for, with Cézanne, they may claim to be the creators of modern art, displaying an even more individual spirit in their watercolors than in their oils.

Apart from a few wash sketches of animals and street scenes, intended usually for lithographs and all done before 1900, most of Bonnard's watercolors were painted forty years afterward in the South of France.

Between 1930 and 1938 Pierre Bonnard painted several watercolors and gouaches on the Côte d'Azur, in which he perfectly caught the luminosity of the Midi, that warm, crystalline light which deadens color instead of intensifying it. *The White Yacht* in the harbor at Cannes is one of that series of very freely painted sketches. What a brilliant transposition of nature! The picture is conceived in a very individual color range: the still white shell of the boat contrasting with the blue sea, while the yellow walls of the houses seem to fade into the green background of the hills. Using a very restricted palette, Bonnard here achieves a rare and unexpected harmony. Looking at this sunlit painting, one is forcibly reminded of Proust's famous description of Elstir, for whom Bonnard may perhaps have served as a model: "Their charm [Elstir's paintings] lay in a kind of metamorphosis of things seen analogous to the poetic metaphor; as if God

the Father had created things by name and Elstir had obliterated it, recreating them under a new guise . . . . Those rare moments when one sees nature poetically, as it is, are the fabric of Elstir's work."

Watercolor and gouache, 12 ⅝ × 9 ½ in.
Signed below on the left: Bonnard.

*Provenance:* The painting remained in the artist's studio until his death.

*Publications:* This watercolor is here reproduced for the first time.

*Private Collection, New York.*

10 *Interior of the Artist's House at Le Cannet* (1945)

This interior, painted by Pierre Bonnard at Le Cannet during the summer of 1945, shows a corner of the dining room in his house, Le Bosquet, which appears in several paintings of this period. Bonnard is here experimenting with the effect of light on objects and translating his impressions through unexpected colors, for instance, red in the shadow and orange in the sunlight, while the tiled floor is at once blue and violet. Everything is transposed. In his choice of colors more intense than those of reality, poetically arbitrary colors, Bonnard successfully solved one of the great problems of his generation. The spontaneous composition of this watercolor is admirable. Seen from outside, the view is, as it were, cut in half by the dark frame of the half-open window, and this unexpected division gives the everyday reality a savor of secret discovery.

Thadée Natanson, in his reminiscences of Bonnard, describes the painter's house: "In the boundless country of Le Cannet the little house, very white inside and gleaming with painted furniture, has retained all the bare rooms still loved by Bonnard; they would be exactly the same were it not for the view from the windows. One can feel at home in them, and especially in the dining room which offers all the marvels to which Bonnard has long accustomed us, down to the tablecloth with its same collection of pottery, glass, and various desserts. Several Renoir prints hang on the wall, and in the garden beyond the French window fig trees, a lime, a pine, a palm, and privets draw a veil over the horizon which so often in Provence seems to lead to a forum. This curtain closes round the table just as the garden beyond encloses the blessing of friendship" (*Le Bonnard que Je Propose*, Cailler, Geneva, 1951, pp. 93-94).

Watercolor, 25 ⅝ × 19 ⅝ in.
Unsigned.

*Provenance:* Bought from Bonnard in 1945 by the present owner.

*Exhibitions:* Collections Neuchâteloises, Musée des Beaux-Arts, Neuchâtel, 1956, No. 183; De Cézanne à Picasso, Maîtres de l'Aquarelle au xxᵉ Siècle, Musée Jenisch, Vevey, 1962, No. 10, reprod.; Chefs-d'Œuvre des Collections Suisses, de Manet à Picasso, Palais de Beaulieu, Lausanne, 1964, No. 129, reprod.

*In the collection of Fred Uhler, Neuchâtel.*

# EDOUARD VUILLARD

11  *Actress on Stage* (about 1893)

Edouard Vuillard was a lifelong enthusiast of the theater. Even as a student at the Lycée Condorcet he made friends with the young Aurélien-François Lugné-Poë, whose ambition it was to design modern stage sets. Hence when Lugné-Poë later became director and producer of the Maison de l'Œuvre, he naturally turned to Vuillard and his friends, Bonnard, Ranson, Sérusier, and Maurice Denis, for the decoration of programs and sets for his avant-garde plays. Alongside this theatrical activity—he was also interested in popular singers and puppet theaters —Vuillard, between 1890 and 1895, drew caricatures of several famous actors and painted a number of watercolors in such bold and arbitrary colors that one might well judge them to have been painted at the height of the Fauve movement fifteen years later. *Actress on Stage*, brilliant, satirical, is a typical product of the stylized manner of the young Nabi. Influenced by Paul Gauguin and by Japanese prints, Vuillard laid his colors in broad, flat washes with no contrasting accent to draw the eye, while the colors are reduced to saffron, indigo, ocher, and pure green tones.

In a book of memoirs called *Le Sot du Tremplin,* Lugné-Poë paints a vivid portrait of Vuillard at the time he was painting *Actress on Stage*. "We tasted peace and contentment at Vuillard's house. Life was nothing if not happy, for Vuillard was effortlessly kind and always effaced himself delicately behind the merits of his admired friends. He lived in the shadows and only as his hair grew white did he reveal the light of his inspiration. Of all these people it was Edouard who from the very first was the most interested in the theater, the best companion, Edouard who often came with me to classes at the Conservatoire."

Watercolor, 9 ½ × 6 ¾ in.
Signed below on the right with the monogram : E. V.

*Exhibitions:* L'Aquarelle en France au xxᵉ Siècle, Galerie Beaux-Arts, Paris, 1962, No. 177; De Cézanne à Picasso, Maîtres de l'Aquarelle au xxᵉ Siècle, Musée Jenisch, Vevey, 1962, No. 235, reprod.

*In the collection of Mme. Pierre Goujon, Paris.*

12  *The Yellow Coverlet* (1896)

Vuillard seems to be essentially an intimate artist, a man talking in soft tones with a predilection for everyday things and the secret nature of rooms. In *The Yellow Coverlet* the painter evokes the apartment in the rue du Marché-Saint-Honoré, where he was living with his mother and sister. One never grows tired of looking at this room, in which every piece is suggested only by the most sparing means and with great simplicity. The young woman, whose face and hair are all that can be seen, has fallen asleep under an extraordinary bedspread, a visionary coverlet reminiscent of an Oriental rug. A picture hanging on the wall, a candlestick, a cup and a bottle on the bedside table complete the furnishings, contrasting with the dark shadow beneath the bed.

It will be seen that Vuillard achieved his perspective in this fine watercolor not merely by following the edge of the table and the skirting board, but by his use of a reddish-brown palette of contrasting tone values. When Vuillard is inspired by the homely atmosphere he loved it is because he knows he is at his best in it. That is the reason "he speaks in a low voice as is fitting for a confidant . . . . Too sensitive to apply force, he charms. There is no attempt to shine, only a search for harmony. The colors seem suddenly complementary, each one a recognition and avowal of the other" (André Gide).

Watercolor, 7 ⅛ × 12 ¼ in.
Signed below on the left with the monogram : E. V.

*Provenance:* The painting remained in the artist's studio until after his death; Jacques Roussel, Paris.

*Exhibitions:* L'Aquarelle en France au xxᵉ Siècle, Galerie Beaux-Arts, Paris, 1962, No. 181; De Cézanne à Picasso, Maîtres de l'Aquarelle au xxᵉ Siècle, Musée Jenisch, Vevey, 1962, No. 239.

*Private Collection, New York.*

33

### 13  *A Saint-Lazare* (1885)

Toulouse-Lautrec, unlike Bonnard and Vuillard, never painted landscapes in watercolor. The painter of the Moulin-Rouge was not interested in nature, the open air, or the play of light and sunshine. His world was humankind. Whether his subjects were drawn from the theater, concerts, the circus, bars, brothels, hospitals, or prisons, he always gave his whole attention to the human figure. In the sketch shown here the artist is less interested in setting the scene than in drawing the main features of his model.

Toulouse-Lautrec painted this wash in 1885 for the cover of Aristide Bruant's popular song, *A Saint-Lazare*. With brush delicately dipped in Chinese ink, he outlines in silhouette the famous song-writer's heroine. She was a fine girl who became a streetwalker, not from vice or laziness, but because she was in love. Arrested without papers, she was sent to Saint-Lazare, the prison-hospital dreaded by the Paris *filles de joie*. Uncomplaining, she thinks only of her lover, now deprived of her resources and in her distress she courageously takes up a pen to write him a letter:

> *I write to you from prison,*
> *My poor Polyte.*
> *I don't know how it happened,*
> *But it was yesterday.*
> *There is a sickness which comes unannounced,*
> *And when that happens*
> *Nothing can save you from being*
> *Where I am today,*
> *In the can at Saint-Lazare.*

Wash, gouache, and blue pencil, 20¾ × 17¾ in.
Signed near the bottom on the left: Treclau (Anagram of Lautrec).

*Provenance:* Aristide Bruant (Aristide Bruant sale, Paris, 1905, No. 1); François Cartron, Paris; Wildenstein Gallery, New York.

*Publications:* G. Coquiot, *Lautrec*, Paris, 1921, p. 216; L. Delteil, *Le Peintre-Graveur Illustré, H. de Toulouse-Lautrec*, Paris, 1920, Vol. 10, No. 10; M. Joyant, *Henri de Toulouse-Lautrec*, Paris, 1926, Vol. 1, pp. 97-98, and 1927, Vol. 11, p. 186; M. Joyant, *H. de Toulouse-Lautrec* (Dessins de Maîtres Français), Paris, 1930, Pl. 19 and 20; E. Schaub-Koch, *Psychanalyse d'un Peintre Moderne, H. de Toulouse-Lautrec*, Paris, 1935, pp. 172–173; G. Mack, *Toulouse-Lautrec*, New York, 1938, pp. 97–98; J. Lassaigne, *Toulouse-Lautrec*, Paris, 1939, p. 14; F. Daulte, *Le Dessin Français de Manet à Cézanne*, Lausanne, 1954, p. XXIII, Pl. 38.

*Exhibitions:* Les Chefs-d'Œuvre des Collections Privées Françaises Retrouvés en Allemagne, Musée de l'Orangerie, Paris, 1946, No. 157, p. 62; Six Masters of Post-Impressionism, Wildenstein Gallery, New York, 1948, No. 35, reprod.

*Private Collection, New York.*

14 *Portrait of Jane Avril* (1893)

In 1893 Toulouse-Lautrec designed the cover for the first edition of *Estampe Originale*, an album containing ten lithographs. This cover shows old Cotelle, a worker at Ancourt's press, working at a handpress, while Jane Avril examines a print. In the watercolor shown here, a sketch for the portrait of Jane Avril, Lautrec has caught the famous dancer holding a fresh color proof. Her attentive face, overpainted cheeks, and mascaraed eyes contrast with her cloak trimmed with skunk and her big feathered hat.

Jane Avril (1868-1923), known as La Mélinite (a powerful explosive), was one of the most famous dancers of the day. Daughter of an Italian nobleman and a Parisian *demi-mondaine*, she made her first appearance in the Quadrille Réaliste at the Moulin-Rouge. Subsequently she acted in many plays, Ibsen's *Peer Gynt*, for instance, and *Claudine in Paris* by Colette.

Looking carefully at the *Portrait of Jane Avril* one perceives that Lautrec's whole art resides in his choice of attitude—the one which reveals all, or, rather, allows everything to be surmised. This is the reason for Lautrec's greatness as a portraitist. He recognizes the telling gesture. And what charm he gives his characters! He brings them to life before our eyes. It is impossible to forget the striking portraits of the singer Aristide Bruant, of May Belfort, of La Goulue and her partner the "boneless Valentin." And Jane Avril, how could one forget her?

Lautrec had the gift of perception and placed his models before us with a sure hand. But their names are of no importance. "By defining so bitterly the marks of time on their faces," writes Jean Vallery-Radot, "Lautrec places them in the human family with all its virtues and imperfections. And it is this side of his art, human and profound, that assures its timelessness."

Watercolor, 19 ⅝ × 12 ⅝ in.
Unsigned.

*Provenance:* This watercolor was sold by Toulouse-Lautrec to M. Scossa; Louis Bernard, Paris; Dr. P. Viau, Paris.

*Publications:* M. Joyant, *Henri de Toulouse-Lautrec*, Paris, 1927, Vol. II, p. 202; W. George, "La Collection Viau," *L'Amour de l'Art*, Paris, September 1925, p. 365; J. Lassaigne, *Toulouse-Lautrec*, London, 1939, Pl. 97; J. Lassaigne, *Lautrec*, Paris, 1946, Pl. 29; M. G. Dortu, *Toulouse-Lautrec*, Paris, 1952, Pl. 35; F. Daulte, *Le Dessin Français de Manet à Cézanne*, Lausanne, 1954, p. XXIV, Pl. 37; P. Huisman and M. G. Dortu, *Lautrec par Lautrec*, Lausanne-Paris, 1964, reprod., p. 101.

*Exhibitions:* One Hundred Years of French Painting, Nelson Gallery, Kansas City, 1935, No. 60; Toulouse-Lautrec, Wildenstein Gallery, New York, 1946, p. 28, No. 19; Six Masters of Post-Impressionism, Wildenstein Gallery, New York, 1948, p. 45, No. 28.

*Private Collection, New York.*

15  *Blue Room* (1920)

The watercolors and color washes of women at their toilet done by Forain toward the end of his career are probably among the least known and most interesting of all his works. At the time the artist was absorbed by the play of light and shadow, the chiaroscuro, dear to the Old Master whom he most admired, Rembrandt. *Blue Room* (sometimes called *The Ankle Boot*) shows a woman *en déshabillé* seated on a low divan fastening her buttoned boots. With rapid penstrokes the artist draws the cushions and the outline of the wainscotting, picking out his model's features as she leans forward; then Forain, who was a consummate watercolorist, skillfully applies his blue wash, which, as it dried, developed an infinite variety of different tones. The light falls directly on the woman's dressing-gown, and she seems to shine, throwing beams into the half shadow, shafts and accents which lend brilliance to the turquoise blues of the materials and the violet tones of the foreground.

René Gimpel in his *Journal d'un Collectionneur* recounts an interesting conversation with Forain during which the artist explained his methods. "The preliminary sketch must be finished; the volumes must be established and definite; mass exists only through light, so how can you later on change your light, which means mass as well? Everything is complementary. These touches, these broad ones, are done on purpose... oh, it is not a method, but a way of feeling. The greatest difficulty is to know when a work is finished, when to stop."

Watercolor, 17¾ × 13 in.
Signed below on the right: Forain.

*Provenance:* The painting remained in the studio of the artist until his death.

*Exhibitions:* L'Aquarelle en France au xxᵉ Siècle, Galerie Beaux-Arts, Paris, 1962, No. 80; De Cézanne à Picasso, Maîtres de l'Aquarelle au xxᵉ Siècle, Musée Jenisch, Vevey, 1962, No. 100.

*In the collection of Mme. Jean Chagnaud-Forain, Paris.*

16  *Tulips in a Vase* (about 1920)

The tulip was Signac's favourite flower. He loved its shapely corolla and rigid stem but was also attracted, as a colorist, by the vivid, singing reds of its petals. The bouquet reproduced here may help one to understand the watercolor technique of its author. Signac has also revealed this, however, in his remarkable work on Jongkind, previously mentioned.

His first principle: when there are two different tones (Signac's palette here consists of four colors: Prussian blue, vermilion red, an ashy green, and a yellow orange), the artist must handle the white of his paper carefully, for "this luminous medium intensifies every tone, complementing its neighbors." Second principle: the painter should place his colors freely and rapidly on the paper, but never superimpose them. "One must not work in stages, there should be no layers, no working in successive coats. Every tint that has been twice painted is more or less flat. Values, from the lightest to the darkest, must be established from the start and painted direct from the palette to the paper. The whole pattern should be strewn in touches of contiguous color, but never superimposed. A sheaf of flowers." Third principle: the pencil drawing should not disappear beneath the watercolor, but be clearly visible, "to introduce into the empty space a play of lines outlining the space to be painted" (Signac, *Jongkind, op. cit.*).

Watercolor, 23⅝ × 17¾ in.
Signed below on the left: P. Signac.

*Provenance:* The painting remained in the studio of the artist until his death.

*Exhibitions:* Signac, Musée National d'Art Moderne, Paris, 1951, not catalogued; Paul Signac, Kunsthalle, Düsseldorf, 1952, No. 67; Paul Signac, Marlborough Gallery, London, 1954, No. 29; L'Aquarelle en France au xxᵉ Siècle, Galerie Beaux-Arts, Paris, 1962, No. 160; De Cézanne à Picasso, Maîtres de l'Aquarelle au xxᵉ Siècle, Musée Jenisch, Vevey, 1962, No. 218, reprod.; Signac, Musée du Louvre, Paris, 1963–64, No. 125.

*In the collection of Mme. Ginette Signac, Paris.*

17 *La Turballe* (1930)

Signac was a sailor from the day when Caillebotte taught him as a boy to sail, to the last cruise to Corsica in the spring of 1935 just before his death. Over the years the artist owned more than twenty yachts and gained a profound knowledge of boats and the sea. At an opening at the Bernheim-Jeune Gallery in 1913 Signac talked about his love for "the long and gentle days spent lazing on board all the different kinds of sailing boats that ply the coast of Saint-Tropez between Port-de-Bouc, Toulon, and Martigues"; he recalled, too, the small ports of call along the coast of Provence, "the landscapes of Poussin, the seascapes of Claude Lorrain, the red rocks of Agay and Le Trayas, the white creeks of Cassis and green slopes of the hills amongst all the blue of sea and sky that is the gulf of Saint-Tropez."

Hence it was through the eyes of a sailor as much as of an artist that Signac handled a subject like *La Turballe*. Signac began by drawing in Conté crayon the outlines of this small Atlantic fishing port—its jetty and lighthouse, the barges tied up along the quay, and the clouds streaking the horizon. Only then did he enhance his pencil line with a Japanese brush, juxtaposing vivid colors in the free space to express the lapping of the waves, the warm brown of faded sails, and the sadness of a gray sky heavy with rain. In this watercolor, as in most of his works, Signac appears really as "a painter of the sea ... of harbors looking out toward the ocean, a painter of boats, their sails buoyant with the thousand colors of hope" (Louis Aragon).

Watercolor, 11¾ × 17⅜ in.
Signed and dated below on the right: P. Signac, La Turballe, 20 aout 30.

*Provenance:* Mme. de la Chapelle, Paris.

*Exhibitions:* L'Aquarelle en France au xxᵉ Siècle, Galerie Beaux-Arts, Paris, 1962, No. 157; De Cézanne à Picasso, Maîtres de l'Aquarelle au xxᵉ Siècle, Musée Jenisch, Vevey, 1962, No. 216.

*Private Collection, Paris.*

P. Signac
La Turballe 22 août 30

43

18  *Sleeping Child in a Blue Dress* (about 1903)

This little girl sleeping on a sofa in the shady terrace of Saint-Clair is the niece of the painter's wife, Evelyne Clare. The painting has a fine range of color, showing Cross at his most successful in catching the contrast between the deep tones of the dress and boots of the child, painted in almost pure Prussian blue, and the soft-colored cushions, rattan mattress, and the white of the paper. If we compare this watercolor with *La Turballe* on the preceding page the difference in the methods of the two Neo-Impressionists becomes clear. "For Signac," writes Isabelle Compin, "the drawing plays as important a part as the color, because he uses brush, pen, or crayon to outline colored areas, to draw the rigging of boats and architectural motifs, curving smoke and the festoons of clouds." Cross, on the other hand, uses only watercolors, placing them on the paper in swathes and broad sweeps suggestive of form. In this sketch of his sleeping niece he employs to all intents and purposes only two tones: blue and an orange-yellow, because, in the words of Maurice Denis, "he prefers to give an impression of harmonious color than of intense luminosity." Indeed, for Cross the sun is not "a phenomenon of light which bleaches and fades color, but a source of harmony that restores natural colors, allowing the most brilliant tones and providing a motive for the most daring color. Cross finds in it a pretext for subtle experiment, an inexhaus-tible subject for the deep springs of his imagination" (Maurice Denis, *Théories*, Paris, 1912).

Watercolor, 6¾ × 9½ in.
Signed below on the right: H.E. Cross.

*Provenance:* Georges Couturat, Paris.

*Publications:* This watercolor is reproduced here for the first time.

*Private Collection, Lausanne.*

19  *Ghardaïa* (1921)

The talent for rapid observation, for simplification, characteristic of both Signac's and Cross's
watercolors is found in an even more marked
degree in the work of Marquet. This artist shows
incomparable skill in reducing a landscape to its
essentials, in bringing out the expressive features
and suppressing unimportant detail. With unerring eye, subtle and with a perceptive sense of
geometry, Marquet places the foliage, bridges,
stone towers, and passers-by in space. Moreover
he knows how to produce the atmosphere of each
landscape, so that even his smallest watercolors
of Paris, Hamburg, or Algeria reveal not only
the season, but almost the hour at which they
were painted.

After 1920, and especially after his meeting
with Marcelle Martinet, a woman of Algiers
whom he married three years later, Albert
Marquet went regularly to North Africa, where
he did some of his most original oils and watercolors. During the winter of 1921 Marquet left
the Mediterranean coast to visit the oases of the
Sahara, spending several days in the Mozarabic
city called Ghardaïa. In the watercolor shown
here, the artist, with the strictest economy of
means, has successfully caught the character of
the old Arab city, the warm, sunlit façades of the
houses clustered round the minaret. Only a
touch of lightly diluted color gives an impression
of solidity to the outer wall of Ghardaïa. Even
the white of the paper takes on a miraculous

light. Moreover, Marquet, with unusual sensi-
tivity, places living figures in the foreground.
With a few strokes he shows the Arabs talking
in groups, standing or seated in the market place.
The warm shadows thrown by their jelabs on the
beaten earth are violet-colored patches, painted
with extraordinary freedom.

Watercolor, 9 ½ × 12 ¼ in.
Signed below on the left: Marquet.

*Provenance:* Mme. Albert Marquet (until June, 1953).

*Publications:* M. Marquet and F. Daulte, *Marquet*, Lausanne, 1953, p. XXVIII, Pl. 30.

*Exhibitions:* Albert Marquet, Kunsthaus, Zurich, 1948,
No. 189; Albert Marquet, Musée Royal des Beaux-Arts,
Copenhagen, 1950, No. 57; Albert Marquet, Maison des
Arts, Oslo, 1950, No. 57; Albert Marquet, Musée de
Bezalel, Jerusalem, and Musée de Tel Aviv, 1951, No. 53;
Marquet, Musée Jenisch, Vevey, 1953, No. 78; De
Cézanne à Picasso, Maîtres de l'Aquarelle au xxe Siècle,
Musée Jenisch, Vevey, 1962, No. 155, reprod.

*Private Collection, Lausanne.*

marquet

20  *Venetian Garden* (1936)

When he traveled Marquet always carried a sketchbook, pencil, brushes, water bottles, and a small paintbox, which enabled him to note down his impressions of new landscapes. The changing effects of light and water interested him particularly, so the canals and ducal palaces of Venice offered motifs after his own heart. Probably, as his wife recalls, "Marquet had thought that he would not have the slightest desire to work in the city that has for so long, too often and in so many ways been exploited by all kinds of painters; that city he now saw as if it had just emerged from the sea before his eyes .... Then the lapping, moving waters, all the barges and boats, and the incredible, almost continuous feast of light caused him to submit, as it were, despite himself."

He went to Venice in 1936 for a week but fell in love with the city and remained the whole summer. The descriptive watercolor we have chosen was painted by Marquet in the public gardens of the Biennale Pavilion. Green, yellow, and purplish tones sufficed the artist to conjure the island city from the lagoon. Like the two people strolling down the quay and leaning over the balustrade, we watch a gondola gliding down the canal and look over to the island of Saint George in the distance with its campanile and the domes of Santa Maria della Salute. Between the background and foreground Marquet has achieved a balance full of surprise and novelty.

His fresh vision and quick execution, which go straight to the essential, have enabled him to impart new life to a subject which had seemed, after Corot and Guardi, to be forever exhausted.

Watercolor, 4 × 4⅛ in. (enlarged)
Signed below on the left with the monogram: A. M.

*Provenance:* Mme. Albert Marquet (until December 1965).

*Exhibitions:* Albert Marquet, Musée des Beaux-Arts, Mulhouse (France), 1949, No. 35; Albert Marquet, Musée Royal des Beaux-Arts, Copenhagen, 1950, No. 66; Albert Marquet, Maison des Arts, Oslo, 1950, No. 66.

*Private Collection, Lausanne.*

21  *Nude in an Armchair* (1906)

While Marquet always considered watercolor to be one of the few techniques that enabled him to catch the most fugitive impressions and to bring home exact and sensitive records of his journeys, Matisse scarcely used watercolor at all. Of course, in the summer of 1905 when he was staying in the Catalan village of Collioure, Matisse painted several luminous aquarelles, their brilliant tones foreshadowing his Fauve style, but these were exceptional. For it is true that during those years when he, Marquet, Derain, and Vlaminck were adventurously experimenting with Fauvism, Matisse scarcely tried at all to explore the possibilities of a simple watercolor paintbox and preferred to abandon entirely the rich fields of Chinese ink and especially of wash drawing, those fundamentals of watercolor which produce the most remarkable effects by the infinity of tone possible in black and white.

Drawings and "Fauve" washes by Matisse usually portray female figures, especially nudes, and the artist always preferred working with a model in the studio to making landscape studies and sketches of street scenes on the scene. The *Nude in an Armchair*, drawn in Chinese ink in his Paris apartment, can be precisely dated to 1906. This drowsy woman seated on a folding chair, a small dog on her lap and her arms raised behind her head in a gesture much loved by the painter, is strongly reminiscent of *La Gitane*, a half-length figure with naked breasts in particularly strident colors, which Matisse completed the same year and which is now in the collection of the Musée de L'Annonciade at Saint-Tropez.

With firm, strong hatching similar to that in Van Gogh's drawings, Matisse detaches his languid nude from the lightly indicated background of the studio. He underlines the ample curves of the young woman with a swarm of interwoven lines, heightened in turn by heavy shadows of wash.

Brush drawing in Chinese ink and wash, 25 ⅝ × 18 ⅛ in. Signed below on the right: Henri Matisse.

*Provenance:* Dr. Heinz Braun, Breslau; acquired in 1944 by the Art Institute of Chicago (Mrs. Potter Palmer Donation).

*Publications:* R. Schacht, *Henri Matisse*, Dresden, 1922, reprod., p. 62; R. Shoolman and C. Slatkin, *Six Centuries of French Master Drawings in America*, New York, 1950, p. 236, Pl. 132; H. Barr, *Matisse, His Art and His Public*, New York, 1951, reprod., p. 322; J. Cassou and P. Jaccottet, *Le Dessin Français au XXe Siècle*, Lausanne, 1951, Pl. 26; E. Trier, *Zeichner des XX. Jahrhunderts*, Berlin, 1956, Fig. 16.

*Exhibitions:* Henri Matisse, Thannhauser Galleries, Berlin and Lucerne, 1930, No. 107, reprod.; Drawings Old and New, The Art Institute of Chicago, 1946, No. 36, Pl. xxviii; Les Fauves, New York, Minneapolis, San Francisco, Toronto, 1952–53, No. 114; French Drawings from American Collections, Clouet to Matisse, The Metropolitan Museum of Art, New York, 1959, No. 202, Pl. 181; Master Drawings from the Art Institute of Chicago, Wildenstein Gallery, New York, 1963, No. 151.

*The Art Institute of Chicago.*

Henri-Matisse

51

**22** *Study for The Dance—Two Figures* (about 1932)

When Matisse was invited in 1930 to be a member of the jury for the Carnegie Prize in Pittsburgh, the collector Alfred Barnes invited him to stay at Merion, Pennsylvania, near Philadelphia, and asked him to make a mural decoration for the three lunettes above the windows in the large gallery of his museum. After some hesitation Matisse accepted this commission. It was to be a mural 170 feet long on the theme "The Dance."

The painter set vigorously to work and finished within a few months. However, as a result of a mistake in the original measurements, the finished work was not exactly the right size for its intended position. Matisse therefore returned to work and composed a second version, which he finished in 1933. When it was finally placed at Merion, Barnes wrote to the artist: "Your painting is like the rose window of a cathedral." The watercolor shown here is a study for the first version of *The Dance*, (which remained in France and is now in the Musée d'Art Moderne in Paris). It is probably a sketch for the two figures occupying the right-hand arch. In a few arabesques, outlining the figures with sensitive strokes, Matisse has successfully caught the airy steps and dancing forms which one hesitates to call dancers, for they are truly abstract. The silhouettes are enhanced with flat washes of watercolor in a brilliantly luminous and vivid yellow.

During an interview with G. Charbonnier, who asked what he thought of Alain's famous dictum that painting expresses time, drawing only the fleeting moment, Matisse replied that he was only concerned with outlining a body in space and that the process was unimportant. "And," the painter added, "I believe that painting and drawing express the same thing. Drawing is painting done with reduced tools. On a white surface, a sheet of paper, with a pen, brush, and ink one can create volumes by use of contrast."

Pen and watercolor, 10 ⅝ × 8 ¼ in.
Signed below on the right: H. Matisse.
*Private Collection, Geneva.*

53

23 *Nude in the Studio* (1904)

Henri Manguin dedicated himself from the beginning to the study of the female form and never tired of painting nudes of ample proportions beside the sea, in a peaceful garden, or in the subdued light of a studio. Reclining, standing, or seated, occupied with their toilet, attentively reading, or overcome by sleep, Manguin's women have no other function than to expose their bodies to the light. All the large Fauve nudes, painted by the artist between 1902 and 1907 were preceded more or less directly by several powerfully descriptive sketches in Chinese ink. In the words of Pierre Cabanne, all these many sketches have no other aim but "to record a tone, catch an attitude, or fix an effect of light enabling the artist to remember these things seen, to be used later in a larger composition.... The painter thus keeps both his hand and eye in, then puts the sketches in a portfolio where he can look at them from time to time, criticizing one, praising another, while a third will remind him of a moment of happiness, wonder, or surprise" *(Manguin,* Neuchâtel, 1964, pp. 40 and 42).

It was probably in his Paris studio that Manguin caught the spontaneous action of his model's lighting the stove before she took up her pose. The artist sets the scene with a few imaginative lines—the bowl in front of the mirror and the crackling stove—and with light brushstrokes catches the movement of the woman bending her fine body before the stove, which is accented here and there by shadows to give it greater relief and define its position in space.

Chinese ink wash, 10 ¾ × 8 ¼ in.
Signed below on the right: Manguin.

*Publications:* This brush wash is reproduced here for the first time.

*In the collection of Mme. Lucile Martinais-Manguin, Paris.*

55

24  *Peaches and Grapes* (1905)

The art of Henri Manguin, like that of Cross and Signac, is closely linked with Provence and the Mediterranean coast, where the painter and his family lived for many years. While staying at Saint-Tropez in 1905 Manguin painted the delicate peaches and muscat grapes in a basket in the garden of the villa Demierre which he had rented for the summer. Skillfully using the white of the paper to separate his colors and thereby liberating their luminous vitality, Manguin achieved the effect of hot sunshine on the fruit lying on the table, perfuming the air of the arbor and giving the scene a kind of domestic somnolence essential to the artist's conception of a Still life.

The painting reveals the difference between Manguin and the Master of Aix-en-Provence, whom he fervently admired. "With Manguin," declared Professor Hahnloser, who knew him well, "every painting is the result of a spontaneous impulse, conveyed untouched onto the paper in one swift movement. Manguin's is always an experimental vision, an impulse arising from a passing enthusiasm, whereas Cézanne's painting is the outcome of repeated studies of the same object . . . . When things went badly Manguin worked himself into an emotional state and, with him, the description temperamental artist is no cliché but a matter of fact. It also had a marked effect on his work, for Manguin's subjects vibrate. His palette lights up by the power of his inspiration" (*Manguin*, Neuchâtel, 1964, pp. 72 and 74).

Watercolor, 14 ¼ × 18 ½ in.
Signed below on the right: Manguin.

*Provenance:* The painting remained in the artist's studio until he died.

*Exhibitions:* Depuis Bonnard, Musée National d'Art Moderne, Paris, 1957, No. 139; Henri Manguin, Musée Toulouse-Lautrec, Albi, 1957, No. 61; De l'Impressionnisme à Nos Jours, Musée National d'Art Moderne, Paris, 1958, No. 139; Gustave Moreau et Ses Elèves, Musée Cantini, Marseille, 1962, not catalogued; De Cézanne à Picasso, Maîtres de l'Aquarelle au xxᵉ Siècle, Musée Jenisch, Vevey, 1962, No. 148; Manguin, Musée des Beaux-Arts, Neuchâtel, 1964, No. 3, reprod., p. 55.

*In the collection of Mme. Lucile Martinais-Manguin, Paris.*

**25** *The Paddock at Chantilly* (1931)

Raoul Dufy was much interested in horse racing even as a young man. There is a *Paddock Scene* dating from 1913 among the Girardin Collection in the Musée d'Art Moderne in Paris. But it was not till later, around 1930, that the artist painted his luminous watercolors on the courses of Longchamp and Deauville in France and Epsom and Ascot in England. Although he occasionally tried to depict the galloping thoroughbreds, it was really the fashionable elegance of the public which drew his eye. In this watercolor Dufy amused himself by sketching the jockeys perched nonchalantly on their mounts and circling the paddocks at Chantilly under the eyes of the owners and their silk-gowned wives. How admirably the painter created, with a few touches of pure color, the silhouetted figures and the movement of the horses. Observing that dark reflected shadows alter tones which are not in direct sunlight, Dufy divided the suit of the man in the foreground, for instance, into two separate parts: one half of his jacket is a purplish blue, the other green, reflecting the sharp color of the grass.

In one of his unpublished notebooks Dufy explains the method of analyzing color and light, as exemplified in his watercolors: "I paint with raw color which produces its own radiance, whereas in reality it is the sun which lights up and makes the colors live. If I had a color-star of my own I would use it to brighten my colors.

But in painting it is my raw materials which make the sun; they are not made by it; in other words, every colored object is reflecting the absent sun, and when it does appear the sun is yellow or white; but you cannot depict different objects with the color chosen to represent the sun, the source of light, but must give the objects, even when they are in full sunlight, their own local and inherent color. It is the harmonious distribution of these light-colors which builds a good composition. Light itself has no particular tone because it is the combination of all theoretical colors."

Watercolor, 17¾ × 24 in.
Signed below on the right: Raoul Dufy.

*Exhibitions:* Raoul Dufy, Musée National d'Art Moderne, Paris, 1953, No. 136; De Cézanne à Picasso, Maîtres de l'Aquarelle au xxᵉ Siècle, Musée Jenisch, Vevey, 1962, No. 87.

*In the collection of Dr. A. Roudinesco, Paris.*

59

26 *The Mediterranean* (1933)

"The sea is an almost infinite source of inspiration for Dufy," wrote Jacques Lassaigne. "It creates new substances and is itself nurtured by a world of inhabitants and symbolic images. He is not interested in the sea itself, but regards it as an endless extension of land, an ideal way to reach the horizon and the larger skies beyond." In the watercolor heightened with white gouache reproduced here, this symbolism is particularly evident. It sufficed the artist to open the windows of his dreams on the sky and the sea to evoke the Mediterranean. Dufy, the magician, called up from the red sand and triangular waves a whole world of fantasy: shells, an amphora, spouting whales, sea horses and, far away, sailing yachts and three steamships silhouetted against the horizon. Yet this apparently easy brushwork, and these fresh, cheerful colors, should not blind us to the intuitive brilliance of his drawing—depicting so easily the broad bands of the lowered blind, the smoke trails of steamers, as well as the huge sea shell, floating on the water, an imaginary vessel for Amphitrite, goddess of the sea.

Dufy tried by subtle simplification, controlled by the different features of his watercolor, "to produce an image, not having the appearance, but retaining the force of reality . . . . I do not believe," he remarks in one of his unpublished notebooks, "that a work in the early stages is part of the realization of a finished plan; the painter has itching fingers when he picks up a brush or pencil and begins to work with no fixed aim, nothing more than to assuage the urge in his hands. The marks he makes on the paper reveal the shape and movement more than these things do themselves; in this way is born the miracle of the transfiguration of the world into images, out of the simple ability of the artist to create them."

Watercolor and gouache, 19⅝ × 26¾ in.
Signed and dated below on the right: Raoul Dufy 1933.

*Exhibitions:* Raoul Dufy, Musée National d'Art Moderne, Paris, 1953, No. 115 (with the title *Marine Decoration*); De Cézanne à Picasso, Maîtres de l'Aquarelle au xxᵉ Siècle, Musée Jenisch, Vevey, 1962, No. 85.

*In the collection of Dr. A. Roudinesco, Paris.*

27 *Carnival Figures* (1906)

Derain always loved carnival scenes and often painted actors of the Commedia dell'Arte, such as Pierrot and Harlequin, and people wearing masks. Like his two great contemporaries, Picasso and James Ensor, Derain was fascinated by masks, painting and even making some toward the end of his life, inspired by actors in classical tragedy. The free and vigorous Fauve watercolor reproduced here depicts the fleeting silhouettes of masqueraders, strolling down the middle of a street at carnival time. With a few brushstrokes and lively spots of color Derain records the couples' swift movements. Punch in a red bowler skips and dances, crossing his legs, while his companion hides her face behind a blue scarf; beside them a man of fashion with a russet goatee and a red walking stick strides at a great pace, dragging along his girl, who flaunts an extraordinary plumed hat and gathers up her skirt as she hurries. Everything is expressed with great economy: Derain has admirably observed his subjects' attitudes, explaining now in detail, or again leaving everything to the imagination. Despite the apparent freedom of touch and fresh, cheerful colors, nothing is forgotten. Every technique "is used in the strictest and yet most expressive way" (Jean Cassou). Fauvism as a movement was too violent to last very long. Derain himself described it as "the ordeal by fire, purifying everything," and towards 1909 every member of the group had found his own path.

Watercolor, 15 ¾ × 21 ⅝ in.
Signed below on the right: A. Derain.

*Exhibitions:* De Cézanne à Picasso, Maîtres de l'Aquarelle au XXᵉ Siècle, Musée Jenisch, Vevey, 1962, No. 58.

*Private Collection, Paris.*

28  *Bathers* (1908)

From May until November of 1908 André Derain stayed at Martigues, a small fishing village near Marseille, intending to work quite alone, far from the demanding and busy life of Paris. As soon as he arrived Derain wrote to his faithful friend Vlaminck to tell him of his discovery: "I am in the South and happier than ever before, quite peaceful in the superb countryside. I left without ceremony and I suppose the gang at Montmartre will be upset . . . . I am going to work hard and become a real painter again. It is very difficult to paint in Paris. One has no point of contact and I think this is the only place where one feels wholly a painter" (*Lettres à Vlaminck,* Paris, 1955, p. 163).

Inspired by the Midi the young artist painted some of his most serene and sensitive water-colors, in which, according to his own statements, he had tried to discover "form shaped by light and air, only to be seen in full light." This preoccupation is particularly evident in this watercolor, which is actually only a blue-green wash, heightened with three yellow splashes, lit by the white paper *en réserve*. Pondering over the example of Cézanne, who also worked at Martigues and L'Estaque, Derain here tried "to paint like Poussin, but on the scene" by including nudes in a landscape. Standing, seated, or crouching, with their flowing hair and curving limbs that harmonize with the curling leafy branches, the five bathers stand out from the hillside and the peaceful surface of the sea, the water bleached by the summer heat.

Watercolor, 16⅛ × 20⅞ in.
Signed below on the right: A. Derain.

*Provenance:* Jacques Doucet, Paris; Paul Guillaume, Paris.

*Publications:* G. Hilaire, *Derain*, Geneva, 1959, Pl. 67.

*Exhibitions:* Derain before 1915, Museum of Fine Arts, Houston, 1961–62; L'Aquarelle en France au xxᵉ Siècle, Galerie Beaux-Arts, Paris, 1962, No. 56; De Cézanne à Picasso, Maîtres de l'Aquarelle au xxᵉ Siècle, Musée Jenisch, Vevey, 1962, No. 59, reprod.; Derain, Hirschl and Adler Galleries, New York, 1964, No. 13; Derain, The Arts Council of Great Britain, London and Edinburgh, 1967, No. 126, reprod., p. 101.

*In the collection of Pierre Lévy, Troyes.*

29  *Crossroads at Montparnasse* (about 1918)

After the armistice in 1918 Vlaminck rented a small studio at 26 rue du Départ, near Montparnasse station. From the window the artist made several ink drawings of his impressions of postwar Paris. "Each district was like a province," wrote Vlaminck in a book of memoirs entitled *Paysages et Personnages,* "every corner had its charm, every Faubourg its color, its customs and inhabitants. The paved streets smelled of horse dung and the air was clearer. There was no gasoline to poison the atmosphere and you could cross the streets and Boulevards without bothering about road blocks, one-way streets, or traffic." That provincial Paris is the subject of this fine wash. In a few brushstrokes, the style recalling lithographic pencil, Vlaminck could bring to life the intersection of Boulevard Raspail and Boulevard Montparnasse in the days before it was overrun by cars and buses.

An advance study for a large oil painting, now in the Bernheim-Jeune Collection in Paris, this urban scene is important not only because it is characteristic of Vlaminck's "Cézanne" period, but because it is one of this artist's rare views of Paris. Indeed Vlaminck soon realized that he did not like living in a town and left Paris, which exasperated him, to return to the French countryside to seek his childhood memories: "A path in the woods, the road, the shape of roads; a river bank with still, deep water, the reflection of a house, the shape of a boat, a house beside a country road, sky with black clouds, sky with pink clouds."

Ink drawing and wash, 15 × 18 ⅛ in.
Signed below on the right : Vlaminck.

*Exhibitions:* Vlaminck, Kunstmuseum, Berne, 1961, No. 205, reprod.

*In the collection of Dr. Sigmund Pollag, Zurich.*

30  *Village Street, Fessanvilliers* (about 1928)

This road passing through the village of Fessanvilliers, near Dreux in the province of Eure-et-
Loir, is typical of Vlaminck's Expressionist style
and of his liking for the industrial landscapes
around Paris set against a stormy sky. In contrast
to pure watercolorists, such as Signac or Marquet, who place their diluted colors side by side,
allowing the white of the paper to show "en
reserve," Vlaminck has here covered the whole
ground with colors placed almost immediately
one over the other, and, in order to bind together certain parts of his subject, especially the
roofs of the cottages and the melting snow on
the ground, has added white gouache. The
snow landscape was taken up by Vlaminck in
1910, after an almost total neglect since the paintings of Brueghel, to become henceforward one
of his favourite subjects. Here the powerful contrast between shadow and light—note the brilliant yellow of the café sign—as well as the sharp
tones of black and white accentuating this winter
scene, enabled Vlaminck to express the desola-
tion of the scene and his own feelings of distress
and solitude. In fact, the artist tried all his life to
penetrate below the surface. "I would look at a
landscape," he said one day, "and receive a vague,
yet precise impression; then I forgot it. Sometimes it would come back to me long afterwards,
but absolutely clearly. Then I introduced it into
the landscape I was painting, hence I paint not
only what I see but something else besides."

Watercolor and gouache, 12 ⅝ × 17 ¾ in.
Signed below on the left: Vlaminck.

*Provenance:* Galerie Charpentier, Paris.

*Exhibitions:* L'Aquarelle en France au xxe Siècle, Galerie
Beaux-Arts, Paris, 1962, No. 175; De Cézanne à Picasso,
Maîtres de l'Aquarelle au xxe Siècle, Musée Jenisch,
Vevey, 1962, No. 230.

*Private Collection, Paris.*

31  *Table with Fruit and a Bottle of Wine* (1957)

Segonzac never abandoned still life, even when he was preoccupied with watercolors of Chaville, Le Grand Morin, or Saint-Tropez. Roger Passeron wrote that "he returns to it with pleasure, whether as an exercise in his research on composition and rhythm or as relaxation from more exacting work." Painted in two or three sittings, Segonzac's still lifes usually represent a table laden with fruit, flowers, or other homely things. The style and brilliant colors are reminiscent of Courbet, and indeed Segonzac, after the fashion of the Master of Ornans, whom he admires, endows his flowers with a rich texture and extraordinary vitality, as if they were fresh from the garden.

Dunoyer de Segonzac painted this southern still life in the summer of 1957 on the terrace of his house overlooking the bay of Les Canebiers at Saint-Tropez. In the quiet of his garden the artist has arranged a bunch of flowers, a bottle of *vin rosé*, three lemons, a jug of cold water, and a basket of golden-skinned peaches on a pink tiled table. These things—seen also in other watercolors—form a brilliant symphony of color.

C. Roger-Marx, Segonzac's most perceptive critic, observed: "He denies the trees, hills, and the sea the expression he is ready to accept from the familiar flowers and fruit of summer's abundance, as if he wanted to show that he too, if he wished, could shout aloud with joy and paint in shrill colors" (*Dunoyer de Segonzac*, Geneva, 1951, pp. 58-59).

Watercolor, 21 ⅝ × 29 ⅞ in.
Signed below toward the right: A. Dunoyer de Segonzac.

*Provenance:* André Dunoyer de Segonzac, Paris; Georges Moos, Geneva; sold by Georges Moos to its present owner on December 17, 1958.

*Exhibitions:* De Cézanne à Picasso, Maîtres de l'Aquarelle au xxe Siècle, Musée Jenisch, Vevey, 1962, No. 94, reprod.; Chefs-d'Œuvre des Collections Suisses, de Manet à Picasso, Palais de Beaulieu, Lausanne, 1964, No. 281, reprod.

*Private Collection, Lausanne.*

A. Dunoyer de Segonzac

32  *The Bay of Les Canebiers at Saint-Tropez* (1960)

Segonzac first turned his attention to landscape in the summer of 1908 at Saint-Tropez when he discovered the austere and solemn beauty of Provence. From the outset Provence attracted the artist profoundly. He found it "very great, very classical and very beautiful." But it was only after 1926 that Segonzac began to spend several months annually in the Midi, sometimes in winter, sometimes in summer. One of the views of which he never tired during his stays at Saint-Tropez is the mountain range of the Maures dominating the bay of Les Canebiers protected by the encircling hills.

This watercolor is undoubtedly one of the finest of the versions so dear to the artist. To paint "*le beau motif*," as he often called it, a lonely little farm hidden among the vines with a row of cypresses following the curve of the hill toward the sea, Segonzac introduced somber blues, glaucous greens, reddish-browns, and violet tones into his palette. This large watercolor, mature and full of interest, is remarkable for the way the ink drawing acts as a framework for the whole composition, underlining in the foreground the lines of newly turned earth, the twisted plane trees, and soaring branches of the oaks.

Léon-Paul Fargue said that Segonzac "seemed to have been born there in Provence between a cork oak and a small clump of reeds." "It is a fact," the artist wrote recently to his friend Roger Passeron, "that I fell in love at once with this district and have been faithful to it ever since. What a marvelous countryside, where every hour seems blessed and especially those described by my neighbor, Colette, when the fresh breeze from the sea wafts the smell of the harvest and the plowed soil over the warm earth."

Watercolor, 22 ½ × 29 ⅞ in.
Signed below on the right: A. Dunoyer de Segonzac.
*Provenance:* Findlay Gallery, New York.
*In the collection of Mr. and Mrs. Boyd de Brossard, New York.*

33  *Woman* (1906)

Between 1904 and 1910 Georges Rouault painted several extremely expressive nudes, using the prostitutes of Paris as his models. Unlike his predecessors, Degas or Toulouse-Lautrec, Rouault never gave his portraits of these women a salacious or daring character. In his cruel, bitter style, "the nude, eternal, universal, replaces clothes that characterize; an individual portrait gives way to a type" (Bernard Dorival). The watercolor reproduced here was painted in the winter of 1906 in a room on the Boulevard de Clichy, which Rouault and Marquet rented so that their models could pose by the warmth of the stove. The painter outlined in the background behind the model is probably Marquet. With powerful and precise strokes, underlining his brush outlines with ink tones and watercolor, Rouault fixed his model in a collected and powerful attitude. Seated on the divan, with crossed legs, her arms hanging beside her, the woman appears self-absorbed. One must turn back to the great romantic visionaries such as Goya to find a similar combination of grandeur and sad humanity.

The powerful, lyrical character of the watercolors painted by Rouault before 1914 has often been misunderstood. "Since my work was unknown at the time and I a voluntary prisoner of Vollard," Rouault declared one evening to his biographer Claude Roulet, "people could say what they liked. There were even imitations and, where I had given my figures a profoundly tragic note, some imitators, with the same subjects, depicted them in a licentious way, which I would not only have been ashamed of, but even incapable of doing" (*Rouault, Souvenirs*, Neuchâtel, Paris, 1961, p. 189).

Watercolor, 23 ⅝ × 18 ⅞ in.
Signed and dated below on the right with the monogram: G. R. 1906.

*Provenance:* Mme. Sylvia Blatas, Paris; René Drouet Gallery, Paris.

*Private Collection, New York.*

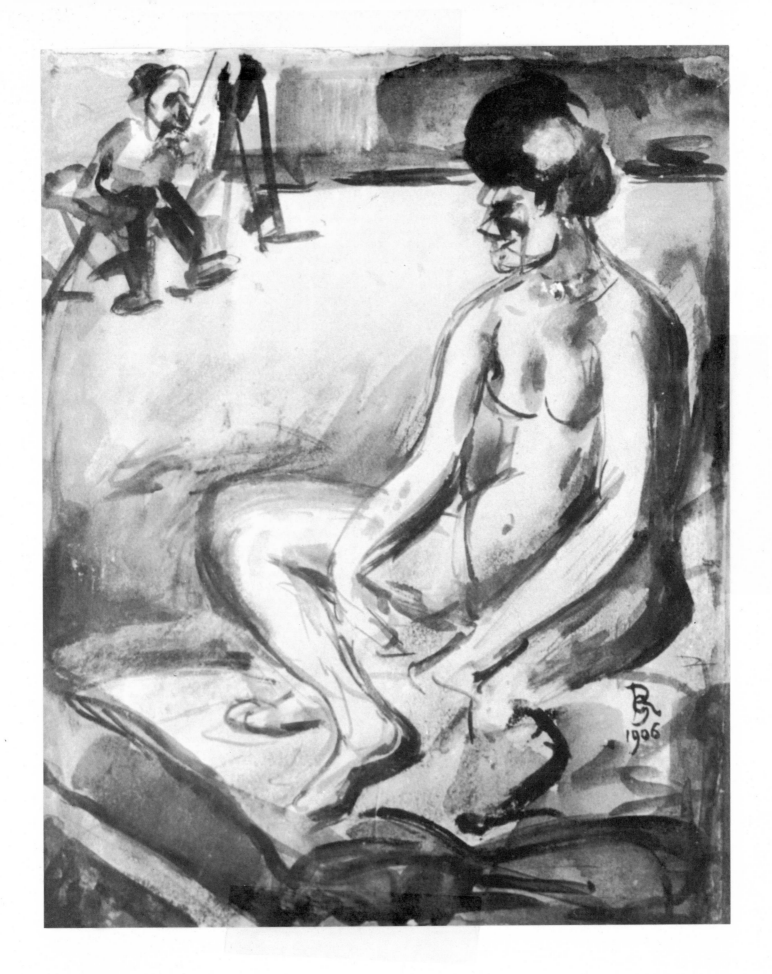

34  *His Honor the Mayor* (1913)

Although Georges Rouault is known primarily as the tragic painter of prostitutes, the illustrator of circuses, and as the author of violent satire on judges and tribunals, he also painted portraits that are grotesque and colorful, vital, direct—reminiscent of Rabelais, or of Molière in *Monsieur de Pourceaugnac*. Rouault was a man of humble origin but he had a satirical turn of mind and between 1910 and 1920 he made ironic sketches of stupid government clerks, pedantic committeemen, the newly rich, fashionable women, and uniformed bureaucrats—in short, people who seemed to him to be the sham characters in the Human Comedy. So Rouault was not taken in by the appearance of power and respectability when he made his rapid portrait of the mayor. He made no attempt to disguise the debonair, yet churlish mien of the magistrate, stout of belly, solidy planted on outstretched legs, armed with pince nez and magisterial gestures. But if Rouault mockingly represents the mayor assuring his fellow citizens in a voice full of conviction that it is he who "makes the world go round and will keep them all happy as long as he is all right," this is not only for the purpose of satire, but for aesthetic reasons—because the mayor wears the tricolor around his waist, contrasting with the faded blue of his suit and flowing tie, and because his stunted figure has a monumental character reminiscent of the most gripping of Daumier's drawings.

Watercolor, 12 ¼ × 7 ⅞ in.
Unsigned.

*Provenance:* The heirs of Georges Rouault, Paris.

*Exhibitions:* L'Aquarelle en France au xxᵉ Siècle, Galerie Beaux-Arts, Paris, 1962, not catalogued; De Cézanne à Picasso, Maîtres de l'Aquarelle au xxᵉ Siècle, Musée Jenisch, Vevey, 1962, No. 200, reprod.

*In the collection of Maurice Coutot, Paris.*

35  *Young Acrobat and Child* (1905)

In the spring of 1905 Picasso found new inspiration in the trappings of the circus and the performers' caravans. That was the period of his paintings of boys in blue, harlequins, jugglers, and strolling acrobats, which express his nostalgia for circus people. In the end Picasso united nearly all his models in one large painting, probably the masterpiece of his early period, *The Mountebanks*, now in the Chester Dale Collection in the National Gallery of Washington. The watercolor reproduced here, in which the scene is set in ink touched with white gouache, is typical of the short transitional period separating the "blue period" from the "pink period." In common with several studies for *The Mountebanks*, the dominant color is pink, and this tone— the color of the young man's close-fitting jacket— and the russet ground colors harmonize with the blue trunks and the gray shadows of the landscape in a subtle and powerful manner. These dreaming young acrobats, drawn together by a kind of familial tenderness, as if the child is seeking and finding protection from his brother, remind us of Appollinaire's acrobats in *Alcools*:

> *Across the plain the acrobats wander*
> *Beside garden walls, in front of*
> *The doors of gray inns,*
> *Through villages without churches.*

> *And the children run on ahead,*
> *Others follow dreaming behind.*
> *Every fruit tree sighs*
> *When the children catch sight of them.*

> *Round and square loads,*
> *Drums and gilded hoops*
> *They carry. The wise*
> *Bears and monkeys*
> *Beg for alms all along the way.*

Watercolor and gouache, 9 ¼ × 7 ⅛ in.
Signed and dated below on the right: A Mlle A. Nachmann, Picasso, Paris 26 mars 05.

*Provenance:* Mlle. A. Nachmann, Paris; Justin K. Thannhauser, Paris, later New York.

*Publications:* C. Zervos, *Pablo Picasso*, Catalogue, Vol. VI, Paris, 1954, No. 718, reprod.; H. Kay, *Picasso's World of Children*, New York, 1965, p. 64; P. Daix, G. Boudaille, and J. Rosselet, *Picasso 1900–1906*, Neuchâtel, 1966, No. XII, 15, reprod., p. 261; F. Daulte, "La Collection Thannhauser," *Connaissance des Arts*, Paris, May 1966, p. 64.

*Exhibitions:* First Showing of Masterpieces of Modern Art from the Thannhauser Foundation, the Solomon R. Guggenheim Museum, New York, April–September, 1965, No. 41, reprod., p. 46.

*Thannhauser Foundation, Solomon R. Guggenheim Museum, New York.*

36 *Faun Playing a Flute* (1932)

In Picasso's work there are two opposing but ever-present currents that developed sometimes side by side sometimes in succession, one concrete, the other abstract. It is a fact that throughout his career the artist has painted works deriving both from the strictest Cubism and from classicism. In his oil paintings after 1925 Picasso abandoned the naturalist vein evident in his paintings of motherhood, monumental nudes, and the harlequins of the 1920s, yet this vein still appears in his drawings and watercolors, as also in the series of engravings for the *Unknown Masterpiece* and Ovid's *Metamorphoses* (1931), in figurative portraits and compositions such as the wash drawing reproduced here. Picasso did this vigorous sketch while staying at Boisgeloup near Gisors in the department of Eure in 1932. In evoking the hairy face of a satyr playing on a flute to attract a wood or meadow nymph, the artist was probably describing his own state of mind. For is it not possible to recognize in the young woman emerging from the shadows, the features of Marie-Hélène Walter, at that time Picasso's mistress, and surely the faun is the artist himself? Whatever mythological disguise he may use, whatever metamorphosis he imposes on his subject, Picasso draws in ink to express his personal drama, his joys and sorrows, his dreams and obsessions. When he recreated the old legends and antique spells, he endowed his nymphs, satyrs, and fauns with a life similar to his own—"a near uncontrollable violence, a cry of despair, something savage, troubling and unquiet" (Frank Elgar).

Hence the artist's watercolors and washes depict, according to his mood, violent scenes or calm, serene images such as the one shown here. Picasso creates the background for the two figures with a few lines and tense curves across his paper and then with small rapid strokes calls up the faces from the shady landscape. Then he touches in the drawing with a wash in a subtle harmony of black and white, which weaves all the mystery of the figures and nature around them.

Ink and wash drawing, 19¼ × 25⅝ in.
Signed and dated below on the left: Picasso, Boisgeloup, 28 oct XXXII.

*Provenance:* Henri-Louis Mermod, Lausanne.

*Publications:* C. Zervos, *Pablo Picasso*, Catalogue, Vol. VIII, Paris, 1954, No. 29, reprod.

*Exhibitions:* De Cézanne à Picasso, Maîtres de l'Aquarelle au XXᵉ Siècle, Musée Jenisch, Vevey, 1962, No. 187.

*In the collection of Mr. and Mrs. Josef Rosensaft, New York.*

37  *Reclining Nude* (about 1923)

About 1923, at the same time as his series of still lifes known as *Les Cheminées*, Braque paint-ed several amply built nudes which were very classical in inspiration. These are *Les Canéphores*, or basket-carriers. They are usually standing, bearing a basket of fruit on the shoulder, but some are half-lengths, seated with a basket on the hip, or reclining, without a basket, like sim-ple bathers. Braque prepared for these large oil paintings by making many sketches in pencil, pastel, or wash, all evocative of the antique goddess of fecundity. The *Reclining Nude* repro-duced here marvelously illustrates Braque's in-tentions: "Form and color remain separate but are simultaneous." Indeed this watercolor is a painting in which the contours of the woman's body—which stand out almost in relief against a black-ink background—are accentuated by penstrokes and sepia touches that do not wholly overlap. After prolonged study of this water-color it becomes evident that Braque achieves his subtle balance by opposing forces. "Braque's black, "writes Jean Grenier," has the force of color; it is not used as a means of carving out a space and accentuating it, but of establishing a sharp contrast in a prearranged plan. The same applies to white, so characteristic of Braque, which he uses to outline and clarify in sinuous lines moderating its impact. 'My art is one of disintegration, not continuity' Braque often repeated. How then is it that his work gives such an impression of harmony ? The answer is that, like all great creative artists, he implies his strength instead of imposing it, and to this end uses the most subtle and delicate means" (*L'Es-prit de la Peinture Contemporaine*, Lausanne, 1951, pp. 83-84).

Watercolor, 7 ¼ × 11 in.
Signed below on the right: G. Braque.

*Publications:* This watercolor is reproduced here for the first time.

*Private Collection, Geneva.*

# JUAN GRIS

38  *The Three Lamps* (1910)

The Spanish painter Juan Gris was nineteen years old when he settled in Paris in 1906. Attracted by the increasing fame of his compatriot Pablo Picasso, he followed his example and took the studio at number 13 rue Ravignan formerly occupied by Van Dongen. Juan Gris contributed for several years to satirical journals to earn a living and, like Jacques Villon, sent illustrations to *Cri de Paris, L'Assiette au Beurre, Charivari,* and later also to *Témoin.* Side by side with this bread-and-butter work Juan Gris painted, between 1909 and 1910, several naturalistic watercolors which formed part of his passionate researches into the relationship between color and form. Most of these are very large; they always depict simple, everyday objects: books, a siphon, vases, bottles, or a teapot surrounded by cups and glasses. Although these sober paintings leave an impression that the artist is still searching, he is nevertheless very close to finding the path he subsequently followed. Just a year later, in 1911, Gris, with his friends Braque and Picasso, embarked on the high adventure of Cubism.

This still life, *The Three Lamps,* is particularly characteristic of Gris' first period, in the simplicity of its composition and distinctive colors, built up from a somber palette of light blues, deep browns, blacks, and grays. In this work the artist not only studied the way different forms are subjected to the movement of light and play of reflections when placed on a white cloth but also tried to stylize the three gas lamps by breaking down their mass into multiple facets, a procedure which he was to apply more generally afterward in his Cubist compositions.

Apart from the series of watercolors done at the outset of his career, Juan Gris later created many gouaches and small watercolors. However, as Daniel-Henry Kahnweiler observed, "they scarcely differ from his oil paintings apart from size and technique. They are never just sketches, but paintings in their own right. They are composed with the same care as the oils, and Gris often admitted that a small watercolor needed as much work as a large painting" (*Juan Gris,* Paris, 1946, p. 220).

Watercolor, 21 ¼ × 19 in.
Unsigned.

*Provenance:* Acquired in Germany in March 1967 by the Berne museum.

*Musée des Beaux-Arts, Berne.*

85

39 *The Pilot* (1916)

During the First World War Fernand Léger was called up as a sapper in the Engineers. All the military machines, especially the artillery and airplane engines, inspired him to paint new works glorifying the machine. "Those four years of war," wrote Léger later, "threw me into a blinding reality such as I had never seen before.... Forced to become an engineer, my new comrades were miners, laborers, and craftsmen in wood and metal. Thus I discovered the French people. At the same time I was dazzled by the sight of the breech of a 75 cannon in the sunlight, a magical effect of light on steel.... Even a closer acquaintance with the reality could not wipe the vision from my mind." In this fine watercolor, also known as *The Aviator*, Léger reduced the principal elements of the composition to stylized and geometric form. The propellers, the body and wings of the airplane, and the pilot's silhouette are depicted in pure colors—blues, reds, and yellows. By introducing several real mechanical elements, Léger "contrasts curves with straight lines, smooth with contoured surfaces, and pure tones with subtle grays," and these contrasts suggest movement and give an illusion of dynamism.

After the end of the war this passion for mechanism grew even stronger in Léger's work, and at that period he produced many gouaches and aquarelles extolling industrial progress. Henceforward, when he painted chimneys, trac-tors, scaffolding, and towns, the artist did not flinch from suppressing all modeling in his work, using only pure tones, a technique that was to have considerable success in the field of advertising after the foundation of *Esprit Nouveau* in 1920.

Watercolor, 9½ × 11 in.
Inscribed below on the left: 30.

*Provenance:* Galerie Simon, Paris; acquired by Hermann Rupf from the Galerie Simon in 1920.

*Publications: Stiftung und Sammlung Hermann und Margrit Rupf,* Berne, 1956, No. 155, reprod., p. 52.

*Exhibitions:* Fernand Léger, Kunsthaus, Zurich, 1933, No. 12 (with the title *The Aviator*); Sammlung Hermann Rupf Bern, Kunsthalle, Basel, 1940, No. 82; Sammlung Rupf, Musée des Beaux-Arts, Berne, 1956, No. 155.

*Hermann and Margrit Rupf Foundation, Musée des Beaux-Arts, Berne.*

40  *Poincaré's Pitcher* (1922)

Roger de La Fresnaye, unlike Léger, who used the techniques of watercolor and gouache for almost fifty years, only learned to appreciate their possibilities during the last few years of his brief career. Gassed at the front during the First World War, La Fresnaye was so seriously affected that he was sent back to Tours to recover; unfortunately he was attacked by tuberculosis from which he never recovered, struggling for eight years against the disease. Greatly weakened, he was forced to rest and had to leave Paris and his friends for the country, first at Hauteville and afterward at Grasse.

Although before the war La Fresnaye had painted very large compositions, such as *The Conquest of the Air* and *Married Life*, which combined the vigor of the Cubists with the spirited realism of a Segonzac or Luc-Albert Moreau, after he settled in the Midi he was forced to limit himself to smaller works : gouaches, watercolor, wax-crayon, and sanguine sketches, "works," as fairly judged by Bernard Dorival, "that do not demand great physical effort or uninterrupted intellectual concentration."

The strange watercolor entitled *Poincaré's Pitcher* belongs to the series of small studies which La Fresnaye could still produce toward the end of his life and in which he took advantage of all the resources of white paper. Wishing to pay homage to the statesman who had fought unceasingly to see that the Treaty of Versailles was fully implemented and who had just been made foreign minister (January 15 1922) after playing a considerable part in the downfall of the Briand cabinet, La Fresnaye was inspired to transpose the naive allegories of Epinal and the *papiers collés* cherished by his friends of the Golden Section.

With great sense of style La Fresnaye placed around the bust of Poincaré several objects and some flowers—all apparently unrelated: a ewer, a plate of crackers, daisies, and an ear of corn; however, he knew how to arrange these in a poetic manner. He not only set the different elements of his allegory on separate clouds, but he also linked them by square bands of black and pink and with tricolored ribbons, curving sinuously round the edge of the composition.

Watercolor, 8 ¼ × 12 ¼ in.
Signed below on the left: La Fresnaye 1922.

*Exhibitions:* L'Aquarelle en France au xxᵉ Siècle, Galerie Beaux-Arts, Paris, 1962, No. 91; De Cézanne à Picasso, Maîtres de l'Aquarelle au xxᵉ Siècle, Musée Jenisch, Vevey, 1962, No. 111, reprod.

*Private Collection, Paris.*

La Fresnaye 1922

# MAURICE UTRILLO

41  *Rue Sainte-Rustique under Snow* (1934)

The reason Utrillo always loved to paint the receding perspective of the streets of Montmartre was that, unlike many of his contemporaries, he saw nature in depth rather than on a flat plane. For instance, in the gouache reproduced here, the brightly dressed women wearing large hats and bustling along the pavements serve less to animate the composition than to mark out the space with points of departure, thus defining the proportions of the houses and the domes of the Sacré-Cœur. Untouched by the art of his day, Utrillo never looked further than the houses in his own district; he is, in the words of Francis Jourdain, "the portrayer of walls." Stone, brick, plaster, and cement were all the artist sought, and with what skill he painted the humble hotels, street lamps, shops, and café fronts of the rue Sainte-Rustique! This gouache, dated 1934, is characteristic of Utrillo's so-called colored style, with vivid blues, vermilions, and slightly acid greens, although there is still an echo of the almost monochrome harmonies of the "white period," particularly in the chilly note of melting snow and the plaster façades of the house, heightened with gouache and crushed chalk, as if the artist were trying to make them seem more real.

Although Utrillo can undoubtedly be called the painter of walls, he is not a painter of street scenes. "He does not look at the passers-by; he sees only the houses. And in painting houses, not men, he reveals his humanity. The outlines he sometimes has to put in (he does it rather badly) are lacking in character and to be truthful are lifeless and conventional" (Francis Jourdain, *Utrillo*, Paris, 1953, p. 9).

Gouache, 19 ⅝ × 25 ⅝ in.
Signed below on the right: Maurice, Utrillo, V.
Inscribed below on the left: Montmartre.

*Exhibitions:* L'Aquarelle en France au xxe Siècle, Galerie Beaux-Arts, Paris, 1962, No. 166; De Cézanne à Picasso, Maîtres de l'Aquarelle au xxe Siècle, Musée Jenisch, Vevey, 1962, No. 233; Utrillo, Cent Dessins, Pastels, Gouaches, Aquarelles, Galerie Paul Pétridès, Paris, 1966, No. 24.

*In the collection of Paul Pétridès, Paris.*

— Montmartre, —                                    Maurice, Utrillo, V.

42  *Girl with Red Hair Wearing a Blue Skirt* (1926)

Pascin's gouaches and watercolors, unlike those of Utrillo, who nearly always depicted the streets of Montmartre, rarely take their subjects from scenes in big cities, or even from nature or landscape. The reason was that this "American from the Danube," as he was called by André Salmon, was concerned only with human beings, nothing else interested him. For instance, when he was traveling during the war of 1914–18 through the United States to Cuba, neither the luxuriant vegetation of Louisiana, nor the immense Texas desert held his attention, whereas he recorded on the spot the white planters and the black workers in the fields.

To tell the truth, wherever he was—Munich, Havana, or Paris—Pascin always sought his models in cheap dance halls, disreputable bars, brothels, and seedy places of all kinds. Hence his work is threaded with a long procession of music-hall dancers, seated or reclining prostitutes, perverse Lolitas, young mulattos in suggestive attitudes, and occasionally even huge nude women, coarsely fat, taking part in imaginary orgies.

*The Girl with Red Hair*—probably one of the many girls who came to pose for the artist in the Boulevard de Clichy—displays all Pascin's mannerisms, described by André Warnod as "writing, but the hand of a man with style." With a few lines of his free-flowing and elegant pen, the artist has caught the pensive mood of the young Parisienne, seen slightly in profile, her clothes in hasty disorder. Then he heightened his drawing with touches of watercolor, reddish-browns, dark reds, and lavender blue, all accentuating the bare breast and bright-colored hair, the folds of her blouse and the somber background. In this fine sketch, swiftly and surely done, Pascin is seen as an authentic heir to the eighteenth-century masters whose taste "for freedom and libertinage . . . for light, delicate, but truly bold colors" he so admired.

Watercolor, 16 ⅛ × 8 ¾ in.
Signed below on the right: Pascin.

*Publications:* A. Werner, *Pascin*, New York, 1962, Pl. 49.

*Exhibitions:* Pascin, University Art Museum, Berkeley, UCLA Art Galleries, Los Angeles, Auckland Art Center, Chapel Hill, N. C., Rose Art Museum, Waltham, Mass., Whitney Museum of American Art, New York, 1966–67, No. 72, reprod.

*In the collection of Mr. and Mrs. Samuel Josefowitz, Lausanne.*

### 43 *The Old Musician* (1914)

At the outbreak of war in 1914 Marc Chagall was in Russia whither he had traveled from Berlin where the dealer and art critic Herwarth Walden had just arranged his first retrospective exhibition in the galleries run by Der Sturm. The success of the exhibition had encouraged Chagall to go home to Vitebsk to marry his fiancée, Bella, who was waiting for him. Almost as soon as he reached his homeland, however, the artist was trapped by the first moves in the war that was soon to become world-wide, and subsequently by the Russian Revolution.

The moment he reached Vitebsk, Chagall found himself plunged into the world of his childhood. His family, his *isba*, the small town streets full of Jews, rabbis, humble artisans, fiddlers, peddlers were all there for him to paint every day. This artist, who, during his first visit to Paris, had been more or less directly influenced by the Cubists and Surrealists, and who had tried to transpose the legends of Russia by applying the rigorous rules of a Braque or Juan Gris and by rearranging them in the antirational spirit of Dada, now set himself humbly to copy the scenes he encountered in the gray atmosphere of the old town of his youth. Excited and happy at his discoveries, the sunshine of Paris forgotten, Chagall began to paint a series of small gouaches and washes describing the life of the people, the small squares and colorful Jewish quarter of Vitebsk. *The Old Musician* belongs to this group of little-known works. It was painted in the winter of 1914 and later used by the artist as a study for an important oil now in the collection of Mme. Katia Granoff in Paris. In the oil painting as in the ink drawing, the artist, by placing a peddler in the middle ground, projected the principal character, the musician, onto a different scale. The old man probably reminded Chagall of his uncle Neuch, who every Saturday after reading the Bible used to play his violin, while the family, especially the artist's grandfather, gathered round to listen. "Only Rembrandt," Chagall later wrote in his autobiography, *Ma Vie*, "could have imagined what went through the mind of the old grandfather, butcher, tradesman, and singer, while his son stood before the window with its dirty panes covered with finger-marks and rain-drops, playing his violin."

Ink drawing and gouache, 11 ¾ × 9 in.
Signed below on the right: Marc Chagall.

*Provenance:* Bought directly from the artist by the present owner.

*Exhibitions:* 20th-century Master Drawings, The Solomon R. Guggenheim Museum, New York, Minneapolis Institute of Arts, Minneapolis, The Fogg Art Museum, Cambridge, Mass., 1964, No. 20, Pl. 25.

*In the collection of Mr. and Mrs. Mark A. Graubard, Minneapolis.*

chagall

44 *Lovers in Blue* (1964)

Since Chagall settled at Saint-Paul-de-Vence on the Côte d'Azur after the Second World War, he has painted more large watercolors and gouaches than at the outset of his career, and these are probably among his best works. Moreover, gouache, a technique in which imposition of colors produces unexpected effects, suited Chagall particularly well, enabling him to give free rein to his cheerfully fantastic imagination. But the usual comment—that Chagall owes his talent as a painter and poet to the vivid images he absorbed during the ingenuous years of his Vitebsk childhood—is inadequate, for none of these would have counted at all if the artist had not been able to express them in pictorial language and re-create them out of his powerful memory. This fine watercolor displays all the symbols of Chagall's world. The characters, like many of those in Chagall's illustrations for Gogol and La Fontaine, are apparently not subject to the laws of gravity. A celestial young gardener hovers above the loving couple so tenderly embraced; he hangs literally in the air, holding out a bunch of flowers the size of a tree. Below, an acrobat with his feet in the air and his head near the ground, is held up by an open umbrella and with his agile movements follows the harmonious curve of the almost reclining, dreaming-eyed girl. The whole scene is bathed in an eery moonlight shining down on the sleeping village, the roofs of the *isbas*, and the church dome. This impression of nocturnal peace is accentuated by the dominant blue of the composition; powerful, yet somber and limpid, it limits every detail, heightening not only the faces of the children hiding behind the wall, but also the withdrawn expressions of the lovers, whispering to each other the words of love composed by Chagall:

> *Once upon a time I had two heads ;*
> *Once upon a time those two faces*
> *Were bathed in the dew of love*
> *And faded away like the scent of a rose.*

Watercolor, 29 ½ × 22 ¼ in.
Signed below on the right: Chagall.

*Exhibitions:* Chagall, Lavis et Aquarelles, Galerie Rosengart, Lucerne, summer 1967, No. 14, reprod. as the frontispiece.

*In the collection of Siegfried Rosengart, Lucerne.*

## 45   *The Dancer* (1957)

Planson was only a boy of twelve when he first became aware of painting, music, and the dance. "The two great events of my childhood happened at the same time," the painter once said, "hearing the Concerto in D by Bach and seeing a Poussin in the Louvre." Quite naturally, therefore, the artist later set out to translate into large color compositions or rapid sketches the atmosphere of the works of Couperin and Debussy. It was also his love of music and his wry interest in every aspect of the Paris theater that led Planson like Degas and Forain before him, to take a box at the Opéra Comique, or to go backstage in the music halls. There he would sketch the ballet in action or ballerinas resting, masks or disguises, Harlequin or Columbine, a prima donna in her dressing-room or Colette Renard on stage.

Examining the many sketches made by Planson in a single evening at the opera one realizes that he was interested only in grasping his subject and arranging a composition which he could reproduce afterward in the studio. In fact, Planson rarely used watercolor as an end in itself, but usually for study and documentation. In *The Dancer*, for instance, the artist has drawn the outline of his model in a few swift strokes done with a very fine brush. He notes the easy grace of the two raised arms crossed behind the head, accenting the profile of the face with the large nose and sensual mouth. Then he heightened his drawing with broad, flat washes to accentuate the curves of the body and to show the movement of the pleated skirt, setting his dancer in greater relief against her background.

Ink wash, 24 × 17¾ in.
Signed and dated below on the right: And. Planson 57.
*Provenance:* Bought from the artist by its present owner.
*Private Collection, Lausanne.*

# ANDRÉ PLANSON

46 *Sleeper on the Banks of the Marne* (1967)

André Planson did not confine his painting to the ballet and the backstage corridors of opera and music hall; he is known more widely as the painter of the river Marne. His landscape, reminiscent of Couperin, La Fontaine, and Gérard de Nerval, is the southern part of Champagne, along the banks of the Morin, Brie, and the Ile de France, where serene hills and valleys peacefully follow the meanderings of the river. He was undoubtedly attracted to Paris but the deep roots which bound him to his birthplace were the most important thing in Planson's life and although he spent long periods at Vaison-la-Romaine or in Brittany, the artist always came back home to La Ferté, where everything and everyone was familiar.

It was La Ferté and the countryside roundabout that inspired Planson to paint the life and landscape he loved in bold, imaginative watercolors. He rarely went out without taking his sketchbook and paints to record the fields of corn and barley of Jouarre, the winding river Marne with its fishermen, boats, regattas, and skiffs, the pleasure gardens of Lagny and the bridge of Dhuys, where the people danced by the light of Chinese lanterns.

Planson would certainly have agreed with Armand Lanoux that "love of a river is bound up with love of women," and so it was beside the water, nestling on islands, that the painter sought a background for his sleeping nymphs, figures as it were from *A Midsummer Night's Dream*, but also for plump and pretty girls and robust bathers taking their ease half-hidden in the reeds. This sleeping nude, stretched drowsily on the grass beside her little Pomeranian dog, belongs to the series of Undines of the Marne and of woodland nymphs ever-present in Planson's work. Red hair beneath a violet cap, petulant mouth and skirt tucked up to reveal firm thighs, she conforms to a type of beauty much loved by the painter—a young, soft, round woman, with graceful supple limbs, half child, half animal, merging with the waving grasses and reflected light.

Watercolor, 9 × 12⅝ in.
Signed below on the right: And. Planson.

*Publications:* A. Planson, *Le Carnet de la Marne* (introduction by A. Lanoux), Paris, 1967, Pl. 12.

*Private Collection, Lausanne.*

47  *Carnac* (1948)

After the Second World War Maurice Brianchon several times spent long periods by the sea both in Brittany and in Normandy, where he produced watercolors and ink washes of surprising vigor and freedom. The artist soon realized that watercolor was the only method by which, with few tones and using a small sketchbook, he could catch the changes in the clouds and sky, the restless waves and damp air of the Atlantic beaches where water acts like a prism and turns into a rainbow.

Unlike Courbet, or the Neo-Impressionists such as Maufra or Henry Moret, Brianchon never tried to depict the "great and sublime" aspect of a rough sea, nor the violence of waves breaking against rocks and jetties, but was more attracted by the peaceful beaches of Deauville, La Baule, Saint-Valéry near Dieppe, or Carnac in the bay of Quiberon. When the tourists had all gone he used to paint the broad avenues along the sea, the wide sands stretching as far as the eye could see, enlivened only by a few late holiday-makers or fishermen at their work.

In this fine wash the presence of the three figures in the foreground enlivens the whole scene, which is familiar and yet unexpected. Using very fine brushstrokes Brianchon was able, with a few rapid touches, to suggest the movement of sky and sea and the values of his seascape—one might almost say the colors, so subtly do the rhythmical contrasts of the ink suggest color, although itself entirely monochrome.

Ink wash, 12⅝ × 13⅜ in.
Signed below on the right: Brianchon.

*Exhibitions:* Maurice Brianchon, Musée des Beaux-Arts, Neuchâtel, 1962, No. 170, reprod., p. 56; Maurice Brianchon, Galerie Beaux-Arts, Paris, 1962, No. 7, reprod., p. 37.

*In the collection of André Guiramand, Paris.*

48  *Poppies* (1950)

Brianchon frequently used watercolor and gouache when he painted the shores of Brittany, the port at Menton, reed-fringed lakes in Périgord shimmering in the wind, and the shady walks beside the lake in the Bois de Boulogne. He depicted also street scenes, fashionable resorts and places of amusement such as the theater, race course, or public parks. Hence the alternation of French cancan dancers at the Moulin-Rouge, and characters in *Fausses Confidences* or *La Seconde Surprise de l'Amour* with the Republican Guard prancing on the field at Longchamp and the bourgeoisie dressed in their Sunday suits on the fourteenth of July, seated before the Mairie at Passy all decorated with flags.

Alongside these landscapes and compositions which are both authoritative and finished, Brianchon produced about 1950 several valuable works in which he restricted himself to a very sober palette—only five or six tones—to produce the effects of light on bunches of flowers. This economy of means and simplicity of style are particularly well seen in the fine study called *Poppies* which formed part of the collection of Richard Heyd, one of Brianchon's best biographers. Here a country bouquet, carelessly pushed into a glass vase, the closed shutters, and the green of the park compose a very delicate symphony. The outline of the objects, drawn with a few sure pencil lines, has disappeared beneath the cheerful tones and watered effect of gray, orange, and pink. "What grace and sure effect we find," writes Claude Roger-Marx, "in the transition from cold to warm tones, in the skillful play of equal values, in the contrasts and relationship of color!"

Watercolor and gouache, 17⅜ × 14⅝ in.
Signed below on the right: Brianchon.

*Provenance:* Richard Heyd, Neuchâtel; acquired from Heyd's heirs on November 15, 1960, by the present owner.

*Publications:* R. Heyd, *Brianchon*, Neuchâtel, 1954, Pl. 4.

*Exhibitions:* Maurice Brianchon, Musée des Beaux-Arts, Neuchâtel, 1962, No. 145, reprod., p. 53; Maurice Brianchon, Galerie Beaux-Arts, Paris, 1962, not catalogued.

*Private Collection, Lausanne.*

# ROLAND OUDOT

*The Road to Maussane* (1956)

Roland Oudot did not start to paint watercolors regularly until after 1952. No doubt the artist had used this technique occasionally as a young man for costume sketches and models of sets, but those were all commissioned for the theater. For the last fifteen years, however, while continuing his studies in the arts of oil painting, drawing, and lithography, Oudot has also tried most of his favorite themes with undoubted success in this difficult field. Although many of the artist's watercolors depict the countryside of the Ile de France, Normandy, or the Landes—regions in which Oudot traveled a great deal—many more tell of the beauty of Provence, its luminous skies, old farms, dry-stone walls yellowed by the hot sun, and hilltops wreathed with umbrella pines.

Captivated by this wild, yet serene landscape, redolent of the spirit of Van Gogh, Roland Oudot, a few years ago, acquired a small farm on the outskirts of Eygallières, a village of the Alpine foothills lying between Les Baux and Plan-d'Orgon. There, without going far from the house, the artist can paint the countryside around him. At Eyguières, at Saint-Rémy, in front of the church of Aureilles, all along the spurs of Les Baux he has made numerous pencil or wash sketches which he later uses as models for larger watercolors. Despite their intensity and vitality, giving the impression of having been painted on the scene, most of Roland Oudot's watercolors are done in the studio and from memory, with the aid of only a few notes and preparatory sketches, which enable the artist to relive the emotional impact of the subject, and which "immediately reveal to him, even years later, the certainty of what he has to do."

This evocative power is displayed in *The Road to Maussane*. The intense gentian blue of the sky, reminiscent of Italian primitives, is here contrasted with the powdery white of a rocky road, striped by cypress shadows, and an occasional farmhouse lost, as it were, amid the tall grasses. It is a scene of stark grandeur.

Watercolor, 13 ⅜ × 17 ⅝ in.
Signed below on the left: Roland Oudot.

*Provenance:* Bought from the artist on November 11, 1957, by the present owner.

*Exhibitions:* Les Peintres de la Réalité Poétique, Salle des Remparts, La Tour-de-Peilz, 1957, No. 135; De Cézanne à Picasso, Maîtres de l'Aquarelle au xxe Siècle, Musée Jenisch, Vevey, 1962, No. 167, reprod.; Roland Oudot, Musée des Beaux-Arts, Neuchâtel, 1963, No. 163, reprod., p. 66.

*Private Collection, Lausanne.*

50  *Venice—La Giudecca* (1958)

Roland Oudot, although primarily a painter of the foothills of the Alps, has also worked in Venice where he has stayed for considerable periods. His appreciation of the Doges' city, the noble palaces, bridges, and canals, soft sky, and everchanging light has enabled him to paint a number of watercolors in the tradition of Guardi and Canaletto.

Even on his first encounter with the city Oudot did not shrink from painting the most famous views: the Doges' Palace, the columns of the Piazzetta, the quay of the Slavs, the church of St. George with its campanile, the Rialto Bridge, and all the baroque palaces along the Grand Canal, their windows gleaming with reflections of the past. But gradually the artist began to venture away from the mainstream of Venice. Confidently wandering through the maze of tiny streets he discovered small homely squares such as the Campo Santa Margharita, brilliant with stalls on market days. Often too Oudot would go and work on the island of Giudecca, formerly the Jewish quarter, where the traditions of the Venetian people continue unbroken, far from the tourist crowds of St. Mark's.

This watercolor shows a view of the St. Giovanni quay beside the Giudecca canal. The building and chapel of the Zitelli institute are in the foreground; the Church of the Holy Redeemer with its fine cupola designed by Tiepolo is in the background. With sure hand Oudot points the

contrast between the centuries-old stones of Venice and the evanescent, ever-moving city of canals. Here the crumbling façades of palaces and there the lapping waves, wooden piles, and black shapes of the gondolas slipping silently over the glaucous water.

In order to give the architecture of the houses a heightened impression of relief, a stronger accent to doorways, windows, and shadows on the quay, Oudot has superimposed several colors, covering now a salmon-pink with a mauvish tint, now a green jade with ashy gray. Using greatly diluted gouache to achieve transparency, Oudot was able to extend the work over several sittings. However, although he has covered nearly the whole sheet, following the technique of pure watercolor, he has taken care to use the white of the paper *en réserve*, thereby lighting up the most luminous elements of his subject.

Watercolor, 17 ⅜ × 23 ¼ in.
Signed below on the left: Roland Oudot.

*Provenance:* Bought from the artist on September 30, 1962, by the present owner.

*Exhibitions:* L'Aquarelle en France au xxe Siècle, Galerie Beaux-Arts, Paris, 1962, No. 128; De Cézanne à Picasso, Maîtres de l'Aquarelle au xxe Siècle, Musée Jenisch, Vevey, 1962, No. 171; Roland Oudot, Musée des Beaux-Arts, Neuchâtel, 1963, No. 176.

*In the collection of Albert Blaser, Geneva.*

Roland Oudot

# RAYMOND LEGUEULT

51 *Hope* (1962)

"I draw only when I feel deeply," Raymond Legueult once told his biographer, Marcel Zahar. "Then when I am really absorbed by my subject, my hand moves rapidly." This desire to let a subject penetrate his mind is found in the watercolors as well as the drawings. Legueult indeed used watercolor as a means to understanding of the chosen subject, to analyze it before painting it in oils in a large composition.

Like many of the Nabis whom he admired, as well as such great interior painters as Redon or Vuillard, Legueult forced himself to limit his vision, to reduce the framework of his daily life so as to be close to the people and things he loved. "One should live as richly as possible within a very small circle," wrote the German novelist Hans Carossa; the words spring to mind again and again when we look at this artist's watercolors. He is a painter for whom there is no place, even behind a locked door, where the attentive ear cannot apprehend the murmuring sound of the infinite. Nothing is so familiar but it can astonish by its mystery.

Hence when he depicts his wife Emilienne on a cane sofa in the studio in the rue Boissonade, or reading with his daughter Anne on the shady terrace of their country house Les "Sorbiers," Legueult is painting the peaceful, happy scenes he loved. Among the themes dear to the artist there is one which reappears constantly in his work: women reclining on the beach at Porquerolles. Of these *Hope* is perhaps the finest. Here intimacy casts a spell. In attempting to evoke two figures in the sleepy hour of the siesta, Legueult tried less to give life to his figures than to submit form to the overall rhythm of his watercolor. The two bathers provide a brilliant splash of color as a counterpoise to other tones. Legueult's fine and sensitive eye discovers tones and new harmonies in the spectacle before his wondering eyes. A few delicate tones, pale blues and flowing pinks, suffice, as they dry into an infinity of small spots, to show the hazy lines of the sea and the sky on the distant horizon. Then he brings the skirt of the woman on the left into relief against a coverlet of blackish-blue and outlines the body of the bather with a fiery red robe, forming an unexpected and exquisite harmony with the ivory sand.

Watercolor, 21 ¼ × 24 ⅜ in.
Signed and dated below on the right: Legueult 62.

*Provenance:* Bought from the artist by the present owner on September 30, 1962.

*Exhibitions:* L'Aquarelle en France au xxᵉ Siècle, Galerie Beaux-Arts, 1962, No. 109; De Cézanne à Picasso, Maîtres de l'Aquarelle au xxᵉ Siècle, Musée Jenisch, Vevey, 1962, No. 135.

*In the collection of Albert Blaser, Geneva.*

III

52  *The Patio* (Mexico, 1963)

While Raymond Legueult scarcely leaves his peaceful studio in the rue Boissonade in Paris except to go to stay at his Normandy farm, "Les Sorbiers," or to visit the beach of Porquerolles, Yves Brayer likes traveling. This is not to say, however, that he is always seeking some imaginary Isles of the Blessed, for he is not attracted by exotic curiosities, but only by truth and humanity.

Brayer loves the Mediterranean and the clear light that accentuates planes and contours; places like Italy, Spain, Greece, Istanbul, Morocco and its oases, the banks of the Nile. But above all he loved to paint southern Provence and the huge stretches of the Camargue, immense plains of reed and salt-wort stretching as far as the eye can see, where men, horses, and bulls live in freedom.

Brayer has, of course, explored other places, but he never stayed long. When he went to the United States in 1963 he paid only a flying visit to New York and then traveled quickly to Mexico to rediscover the southern atmosphere in that ancient land, which bears the marks of the Spanish conquest combined with those of earlier peoples.

Accompanied by his wife and two friends, Brayer journeyed some 5000 or 6000 miles by car, painting many watercolors that pulse with vigor and sunshine. Most of them were done on large sketching blocks and thin paper, and the artist always worked straight from the subject, very rapidly so as to retain his first impression.

On the high plateaus and in the scorching plains of the coast Brayer has successfully translated the Mexican light, which seems to enhance color instead of subduing it, painting the buildings with delicate, typically Indian tones. With his powerfully evocative style Brayer depicts not only the land, but also the markets and festivals of modern Mexico, beggars and mule drivers, the Puebla streets and the motley cathedral of Taxco, the processions of Guadalupe, fishermen drying their nets on the banks or out on the lake of Patzcuaro. He describes, too, the silence of a patio in the evening light, a cool haven for harassed pilgrims. In this limpid watercolor everything is imbued with the simplicity of life: the native in his embroidered cloak, pigeons pecking in the courtyard, the orange tree laden with fruit, and the rhododendrons in flower beside the bubbling fountain.

Watercolor, 16⅛ × 20½ in.
Signed below on the right: YVES BRAYER.

*Publications:* J. Giono, *Yves Brayer*, Paris, 1966, reprod., p. 75.

*Exhibitions:* Yves Brayer, Galerie de Paris, Paris, 1964, No. 16, p. 18.

*Private Collection, Paris.*

53  *Rome—View of the Capitol* (1965)

Georges Rohner was already fifty years old when he discovered Rome, though for a long time he had wanted to visit the papal and imperial city which he knew well from photographs and his classical studies. However it was not until the late summer of 1965 that the artist was able to stay in the capital for the first time in an old house built among the ruins of Trajan's forum.

Rohner was captivated by all that he saw. "A majestic city, a city of stone"—these were the two aspects of Rome which struck the artist most during his walks. The squares and fountains, the Coliseum and the arch of Constantine, the Porta Maggiore, the Pantheon, and the Forum of Augustus, the banks of the Tiber, Bernini's colonnade and Saint Peter's all fascinated Rohner equally, whether classical ruins or the noble monuments of the baroque. He sketched unremittingly in watercolors, and one day, wanting to see over the whole city, stopped to sketch on the Capitoline Hill.

From there he drew the curves of roofs and cupolas against the sky and the wooded hills crowned with umbrella pines. He then placed his watercolors on the sheet, laying them on broadly in a wash, coloring with unerring eye the façades of the houses in tones of ocher, bister and pink, so that they form a gentle symphony interspersed with the blacks of the loggias and the bluish accents of church domes and palaces.

Watercolor, 9 ½ × 12 ½ in.
Signed below on the right: G. Rohner.

*Publications:* G. Rohner, *Le Carnet de Rome* (introduction by P. du Colombier), Paris, 1966, Pl. 1.

*Exhibitions: See* Rome par Rohner, Galerie de Paris, 1967, No. 31, reprod., p. 21. This is a large painting, 36⅜ × 57 ½ in., for which the watercolor shown here is a preparatory study.

*Private Collection, Paris.*

g. Rohner

# MICHEL CIRY

Michel Ciry started to paint in watercolor only after 1960 and from the outset succeeded in imparting new inspiration to a most difficult medium. In contrast to the pure watercolorists —Dufy or Signac, for example—who prefer to add only individual, carefully selected touches of color to their paper and are careful to leave the white between, Michel Ciry, in the manner of Segonzac or Roland Oudot, covers the paper all over, even correcting his original work with immediate additions.

Michel Ciry believes that the expression of space is the essential point of a landscape painter's work, the part which is his alone and cannot be taken from him. Therefore during the last few years the artist has devoted a large part of his study of watercolor to the most austere districts of Spain, those vast and rocky plateaus where the sun scorches the earth, burns mens' skin, and bleaches the façades of the houses. The view of Segovia reproduced here, like those Ciry painted of Toledo and the Tagus gorge, is characterized by an impression of ordered grandeur, a sense of disengagement with the horizon and equilibrium. The painter has used a very somber palette to depict the movement of the hills, the checkered effects of roads and houses and dark patches of olive trees, while the curves of the land reveal the stony ground beneath a thin sprinkling of earth, and the towers and steeples of the ancient city of Castille stand out in the distance against a cloudy sky.

It will be observed that Ciry did not try, as he was wont in the beginning, to fix his composition with pen and ink before applying a wash. Since he learned that ink contains aniline which may change a color, he has outlined his setting in black pencil, painting over this light framework and relying on his watercolors alone for effect.

Watercolor, 28 ¾ × 41 ¾ in.
Signed and dated below on the right : Segovia MICHEL CIRY 66.

*Exhibitions:* Michel Ciry, Peintures, Aquarelles, Dessins, Galerie de Paris, Paris, 1966, No. 54, reprod., p. 36.

*Private Collection, Lausanne.*

117

# THE TECHNIQUE OF WATERCOLOR

*Materials*

All the watercolors reproduced here were painted with relatively simple, almost identical materials which must be broadly described. For if one is to appreciate the subtle charm of twentieth-century watercolors, sepias, and gouaches it is surely necessary to know how and with what materials they were done. The tools of the watercolor painter are essentially a drawing book or block, sheets of paper, pencils, brushes, a small, soft sponge, a box of paints and, for working outdoors, a folding stool and an umbrella so that comfort is assured.

The paper used by contemporary painters is nearly always fine-grained, nonabsorbent, and as white as possible to allow maximum intensity of color. Since it is often difficult to find English papers of the quality of Watmann, French papers are more often used, sometimes slightly rough-grained, Canson, for instance, or Ingres, Arches, or Montgolfier. Gouache painters prefer Bristol board, which is thicker and smoother.

Certain watercolorists start by soaking the whole surface of the paper and stretching it on a drawing board or pad, sticking down the edges. Others paint directly into a sketchbook or on leaves set in a block, which they tear off one by one, fixing them on the board with metal clips or pegs, which are better than drawing pins, as these leave marks on the paper.

For the preliminary sketch and outline of the composition most artists use a pencil, sometimes graphite, silverpoint, Conté crayon, or charcoal, occasionally pen and Chinese ink. Even though this preliminary drawing often disappears almost completely beneath the colors it can also contribute to the general effect, forming a frame on which the colors are hung. Toulouse-Lautrec, for example, touches the color in only very lightly on a sharply drawn sketch. "Cézanne points up, with soft touches of his Conté crayon, the contrasts and tones in the mass that he intends to study." [1]

Once the scene is set, the artist proceeds to the watercolor proper. He uses a small tin box of paints, white on the inside, black outside. The box has two folding covers and is divided into small pans containing hard colors. Each lid is molded to form a shallow bowl for mixing colors as on a palette.

Watercolors are composed of the same pigments as oil colors, but they are mixed with gum arabic to make them adhere. Painters used to mix their own colors with the gum, often adding honey to preserve the suppleness and moisture of the paint. Nowadays, however, painters are able to buy ready-made and convenient materials in which the gum arabic is replaced by synthetic products and the honey by glycerin.

Most painters, when they work in the open air, try to avoid bulky materials and therefore use hard colors and a tin paintbox, but it is difficult to prevent these paints from drying out. Hence, when working in the studio, many painters prefer to use tubes of color which can be spread on the palette in quantities small enough to ensure a sufficiently moist condition.

1. P. Signac, *op. cit.*, p. 110.

YVES BRAYER

55 *A Corner of the Studio* (1967)

Beside the high window of his studio in rue Monsieur-le-Prince, Yves Brayer has made a composition of his painter's tools. On his sketchbook—a horse in the Camargue grasses can be seen on the right-hand page—the artist has placed his tin paintbox with its square pans of English colors. The small faïence vase, clear-cut before the half-open window, is filled with brushes of all sizes, both Japanese and French. A mug of fresh water for mixing his colors is on the left of the vase and on the right a glass of slightly dirty water for mixing his favourite grays. In front of this glass the artist has placed a sponge for wetting the paper or erasing, pegs as clips, and a rag for drying and cleaning the brushes. To the right in the foreground is a rubber or scraper, a penknife, and two brushes, one round and full for painting broad washes, the other finer for more precise and firmer lines.

Ink drawing, 17¾ × 15 in.
Signed below on the right: YVES BRAYER.
*Private Collection, Paris.*

Yves Brayer

To put his colors on the white surface the watercolorist uses a brush, which should be pliant, springing quickly back into shape when lifted from the paper. It should also retain its point when soaked in water. The best type of brush is made of dark or light marten—Canadian is the most desirable—or of squirrel. Apart from his brushes, the painter also needs at least two glasses, one for clear water used for mixing tones on the palette, the other for washing brushes. When working outdoors, a small water bottle, holding about a half pint, and two tin pans, one for mixing the colors, the other for cleaning the brushes, are usually sufficient.

Usually the artist mixes his colors on the palette, but this can also be done directly onto the paper adding a fresh color over one already present while it is still wet. This is a particularly delicate operation, and as François Fosca puts it: "The artist must be absolutely sure of the reactions of his colors on the paper, as it is essential for him to know how quickly they dry. If a color is to be placed over another it must be done at exactly the right moment, neither twenty seconds too soon, nor twenty seconds too late, at the precise moment when the first color is in the desired condition. Should it prove too wet the second color will dissolve into it; if too dry the result will appear hard and lacking in fluidity." [2]

Because its principal qualities are delicacy and transparency, watercolor demands of its expo-

2. F. Fosca, *La Peinture qu'est-ce que c'est?* Aux Portes de France, Porrentruy, 1947, p. 91.

nents decisiveness and speed in the handling of the colors. In other words, corrections, second thoughts, or any kind of change are prohibited. However, by using either a brush lightly charged with water or a fine sponge, the artist can remove a spot from the paper or erase a false tone, but the paper must be sponged very lightly, taking care not to spoil the surface by rubbing, which would cause the color placed by the artist over the former color to be dull and lifeless.

## Methods

Such are the materials used by twentieth-century artists from Cézanne to the present day in painting the works reproduced in this book. The materials are almost always identical whatever the process. The four best known methods are: wash, sepia, watercolor (proper), and gouache.

*Wash* is the simplest stage of watercolor: painting with water, using the white of the paper for highlights. To paint a wash almost always means to enhance a linear drawing with a brush loaded with Chinese ink diluted in water. Chinese ink is known to be composed of carbon and gum arabic: it is indelible and ineradicable. The artist may use colors other than Chinese ink—indigo, for example, green, carmine, or sanguine—but a wash, in the usual sense of the term, consists of a single monochrome.

*Sepia* replaced bister in the nineteenth century

and is often confused with it. It is also a method of watercolor painting in monochrome. While bister is made from wet soot, giving a luminous, warm, golden-brown, sepia, made from color extracted from the bladder of the cuttlefish, is of a darker, colder tone. Color merchants now sell sepia and Chinese ink in tubes, semisolid but soft and easy to dilute.

*Watercolor or aquarelle* (Latin, *aquarella*, watercolor painting) is basically a wash in which several colors are used. Like sepia and plain wash, this method employs no white. The part

56  GEORGES ROHNER: *Architecture* or *the Tools of Wash Drawing* (1967). Ink wash, 10⅝ × 15 in. *Private Collection, Paris.*

played by white pigment in oil painting is taken here by the white of the paper, either *en réserve* or shining through the translucent colors. As has been mentioned, the medium of watercolor is gum arabic or synthetic substitutes. Some artists use aniline, which imparts brilliance to their work.

*Gouache* is a kind of white paste composed of white lead or zinc white mixed with gum arabic, which dissolves easily in water. In contrast to true watercolor, gouache does not use the white of the paper, but powdered white. While an aquarelle is delicate and translucent, gouache is heavier and opaque. Retouching a watercolor is to be avoided, whereas with gouache it is pos-sible to return to a color after it is completely dry as long as this is done in the same tone so as to lighten or intensify the base color. This possibility of superimposing tones had a strong attraction for such painters as Segonzac, Chagall, and Oudot, who all often used gouache while still making use of the white background as in true watercolor. These masters would probably agree with the apt words of François Fosca: "The best way to use gouache is not in thick layers, but heavily diluted with water, almost transparent, a method which falls midway between watercolor and normal gouache." [3]

3. F. Fosca, *op. cit.*, p. 92.

# BIOGRAPHIES

## PAUL CÉZANNE

Born January 19, 1839, at Aix-en-Provence; died October 22, 1906, also at Aix. The son of a banker, Cézanne studied at the Bourbon College at Aix, where he formed a close friendship with another pupil, Emile Zola. The young man went to Paris in 1861, determined to devote his life to painting, and there met Guillaumin and Camille Pissarro at the Swiss Academy. Pissarro introduced him to the future Impressionists and their leader, Edouard Manet. In 1873 Cézanne went to Auvers-sur-Oise with Pissarro and forced himself to attempt an Impressionist technique in landscape, although never neglecting the structure of planes and volumes. Cézanne took part in the first Impressionist exhibition in the following year and again the third in 1877. Unfortunately, of all those who exhibited, Cézanne's work was singled out for the most harmful criticism. Deeply hurt, the painter refused to exhibit with his friends again and retired, barely forty years old, to almost complete isolation in Aix. However, Cézanne is not a true Impressionist but a pioneer who opened up new paths for modern art. Toward the end of his life he had the satisfaction of knowing that a few connoisseurs recognized the greatness of his work and that young painters looked upon him as a master.

*Paul Cézanne*

*Bibliography:* E. Bernard, *Paul Cézanne*, Les Hommes d'Aujourd'hui, Paris, 1892; L. Venturi, *Cézanne, Son Art, Son Œuvre*, Paul Rosenberg, Paris, 1936; A. Chappuis, *Dessins de Cézanne*, Chroniques du Jour, Paris, 1938; B. Dorival, *Cézanne*, Tisné, Paris, 1948; J. Rewald, *Cézanne, Carnets de Dessins*, Paris, 1951; G. Schmidt, *Aquarelles de Paul Cézanne*, Holbein, Basel, 1952; M. Raynal, *Cézanne*, Skira, Geneva, 1954.

## PIERRE BONNARD

Born October 3, 1867, at Fontenay-aux-Roses (Seine); died January 23, 1947, at Le Cannet. After attending courses at the Ecole des Beaux-Arts and the Julian Academy, Pierre Bonnard began to earn his living by making posters and lithographs, which earned him the nickname "Japonard" for his taste for decoration. Acquainted with Edouard Vuillard, K.-X. Roussel, Maurice Denis, and Ranson, he joined the Nabis in 1889 and exhibited with them. After 1900 Bonnard broke away from the Nabis and began to develop a more colorful style influenced by Impressionism. Between 1907 and 1911 Bonnard traveled to Belgium, Holland, and Italy, England, Spain, and Tunisia. Shortly before the First World War he bought a small house called "Ma Roulotte," at Vernon (Eure). From then until 1938 he arranged his life so as to pass the summer in Paris and Vernon and the winter in the Midi. From 1940 until his death Bonnard lived almost as a recluse, isolated from the world and publicity, in his villa called "Le Bosquet," above Cannes.

*Pierre Bonnard*

*Bibliography:* F. Fosca, *Bonnard*, Kundig, Geneva, 1919; L. Werth, *Bonnard*, Crès, Paris, 1919; J. Rewald, *Pierre Bonnard*, The Museum of Modern Art, New York, 1948; T. Natanson, *Le Bonnard que Je Propose*, Cailler, Geneva, 1951; C. Roger-Marx, *Bonnard, Lithographe*, Sauret, Monte Carlo, 1952; A. Terrasse, *Bonnard*, Skira, Geneva, 1964; A. Vaillant, *Bonnard*, Ides et Calendes, Neuchâtel, 1965; J. and H. Dauberville, *Catalogue Raisonné de l'Œuvre Peint de Bonnard*, Vol. 1, Bernheim-Jeune, Paris, 1966; J. Bouret, *Bonnard—Séductions*, La Bibliothèque des Arts, Lausanne-Paris, 1967; A. Terrasse, *Bonnard*, Gallimard, Paris, 1967.

## EDOUARD VUILLARD

Born November 11, 1868, at Cuiseaux (Saône-et-Loire); died June 21, 1940, at La Baule (Loire-Inférieure). In 1884 while studying at the Lycée Condorcet he made friends with K.-X. Roussel, his future brother-in-law, who aroused his interest in painting. The two

*Edouard Vuillard*

*Henri de Toulouse-Lautrec*

young men worked at first in the Maillard Studio, and one of their friends, A.-F. Lugné-Poë, himself a future director of the Théâtre de l'Œuvre, introduced them to Maurice Denis. In turn Denis put them in touch with Bonnard, who took them with him to the Julian Academy. From 1894 to 1914 Vuillard painted large decorative panels commissioned by collectors such as the Natansons, Dr. Waquez, the novelist Claude Anet, Princesse Antoine Bibesco, and the Bernheim-Jeune Gallery. Although he later decorated public buildings (the Palais de Chaillot in 1937 and the Palais des Nations at Geneva in 1938), he chiefly devoted his talents to portraits of middle-class people, especially after 1930.

*Bibliography:* J. Salomon, *Vuillard*, Albin Michel, Paris, 1945; C. Roger-Marx, *Vuillard et Son Temps*, Arts et Métiers Graphiques, Paris, 1945; A. Chastel, *Vuillard*, Floury, Paris, 1946; C. Roger-Marx, *L'Œuvre Gravé de Vuillard*, Sauret, Monte Carlo, 1948; J. Salomon, *Auprès de Vuillard*, La Palme, Paris, 1953; J. Salomon, *12 Pastels de Vuillard*, La Bibliothèque des Arts, Paris, 1966.

## HENRI DE TOULOUSE-LAUTREC

Born November 24, 1864, at Albi; died September 9, 1901, in the Château of Malromé (Gironde). Born into an old and noble family, Lautrec, a keen horseman and huntsman, was apparently destined to lead the life of a distinguished aristocrat, but at the age of thirteen he had a bad accident and was seriously injured in both legs. During his long hours of forced inactivity Lautrec began to draw. The friendship and influence of a painter of horses, René Princeteau, of John Lewis Brown, and of Jean-Louis Forain led him to the Ecole des Beaux-Arts. He subsequently worked in Léon Bonnat's studio and after 1883 with Fernand Cormon, where he met Vincent Van Gogh and Emile Bernard. But Lautrec soon abandoned his teachers to follow his own ideas and inspiration and settled in Montmartre. During that time he often went to the Moulin-Rouge, the Chat-Noir, and other fashionable cabarets, where he painted and drew the stars of the café-concert: Yvette Guilbert, Aristide Bruant, La Goulue, Jane Avril, and Marcelle Lender. About 1896 Lautrec became interested in the women living in the brothels of the rue d'Amboise and the rue des Moulins. Although he traveled to Holland and to London with his friend Maurice Joyant, he preferred to live in Paris, because he was preoccupied with man rather than nature.

*Bibliography:* M. Joyant, *Henri de Toulouse-Lautrec*, 2 vols., Floury, Paris, 1926–27; F. Jourdain and J. Adhémar, *Toulouse-Lautrec*, Tisné, Paris, 1952; J. Lassaigne, *Lautrec*, Skira, Geneva, 1953; F. Gauzi, *Lautrec et Son Temps*, La Bibliothèque des Arts, Paris, 1954; H. Perruchot, *Toulouse-Lautrec*, Hachette, Paris, 1958; P. Huisman and M. G. Dortu, *Lautrec par Lautrec*, Edita, Lausanne –La Bibliothèque des Arts, Paris, 1964.

## JEAN-LOUIS FORAIN

*Jean-Louis Forain*

Born October 23, 1852, at Reims (Champagne); died July 11, 1931, in Paris. While still a student at the Ecole des Beaux-Arts in Paris, Forain spent much time copying the masters and in particular Rembrandt, whom he greatly admired. After the war of 1870 he met in the café called La Nouvelle-Athènes in Montmartre several older artists—the engraver Desboutins, Claude Monet, and Edgar Degas. After early struggles Forain became known for his caricatures and for many years contributed to satirical journals such as *Le Rire, La Cravache, La Revue Illustrée, La Vie Parisienne,* and *Le Figaro.* But Forain's success as an engraver and illustrator should not allow us to forget his work as a painter in oils and watercolor, where his power of observation and depiction of character are reminiscent of Honoré Daumier.

*Bibliography:* M. Guérin, *J.-L. Forain, Lithographe*, Paris, 1910; M. Guérin, *Forain, Aquafortiste*, Paris, 1912; J.-E. Blanche, *Forain*, Essais et Portraits, Paris, 1912; A. Alexandre, *Forain tel qu'Il Fut*, La Renaissance de l'Art Français, Paris, 1931; C. Kunstler, *Forain*, Paris, 1931.

*Paul Signac*

## PAUL SIGNAC

Born November 11, 1863, in Paris; died August 15, 1935, also in Paris. Paul Signac studied for a while with the free Academy Bin and then joined the Impressionists after an introduction by Guillaumin, who noticed him painting by the quays on the Seine. In December 1884 Signac exhibited four paintings at the first exhibition of the Indépendants in company with Georges Seurat, H.-E. Cross, Angrand, and Odilon Redon. From that date Signac faithfully showed each year in the Salon des Indépendants, whose president he was from 1908 to 1934. A close friend of Seurat and Cross, Signac was among the first to adopt the technique of Pointillism, and in 1899 published his book *D'Eugène Delacroix au Néo-Impressionnisme*, a comprehensive explanation of the new school. Signac was fascinated by the sea throughout his life and was almost as much a sailor as a painter. He owned a yacht on which he made numerous cruises to the coast of Brittany and to Provence, Venice, Genoa, Rotterdam, and even Istanbul. It was during one of these voyages in 1892 that Signac discovered the port and village of Saint-Tropez, where he bought the villa called "La Hune." Afterward he stayed there every summer until his death.

*Bibliography:* L. Cousturier, *Signac*, Crès, Paris, 1922; G. Besson, *Signac*, Rombaldi, Paris, 1935; F. Fénéon, *Œuvres*, Gallimard, Paris, 1948; G. Besson, *Signac*, Braun, Paris, 1950; G. Besson, *Signac – Dessins*, Braun, Paris, 1950; M. T. Lemoyne de Forges, *Catalogue de l'Exposition Signac*, Musée du Louvre, Paris, 1963.

*Henri-Edmond Cross*

## HENRI-EDMOND CROSS

Born May 20, 1856, at Douai; died May 16, 1910, at Saint-Clair near Le Lavandou (Var). Henri-Edmond Cross began to study to be a painter at the Ecole des Beaux-Arts in Lille. In 1878 he came to Paris where he worked in the studios of Dupont-Zipcy and François Bonvin. The latter advised him to change his family name from Delacroix, to Cross, probably in memory of his mother, an Englishwoman. From the moment of his participation in the Salon des Indépendants in 1884 Cross was a member of the Neo-Impressionist movement led by his friends Seurat and Signac. Cross, who suffered from severe rheumatism, left Paris in 1891 to settle in the Midi, first at Cabassou in the Esterel, then near Le Lavandou. Apart from two journeys to Italy, one to Venice in 1903, the other to Tuscany and Rome in 1908, both of which were the inspiration for many sketches in watercolor, Cross scarcely left his much-loved property at Saint-Clair, where he died of cancer at the early age of fifty-four.

*Bibliography:* L. Cousturier, *H.-E. Cross*, Crès, Paris, 1932; M. de Saint-Clair (Mme. Maria van Rysselberghe), *Galerie Privée*, Gallimard, Paris, 1947; F. Fénéon, *Œuvres*, Gallimard, Paris, 1948; H.-E. Cross, *Carnet de Croquis* (Introduction by J. Rewald), Berggruen, Paris, 1959; J. Rewald, *Le Post-Impressionnisme de Van Gogh à Gauguin*, Albin-Michel, Paris, 1961; I. Compin, *H.-E. Cross*, Quatre-Chemins Editart, Paris, 1964.

*Albert Marquet*

## ALBERT MARQUET

Born March 27, 1875, at Bordeaux; died June 14, 1947, in Paris. Albert Marquet studied at the Lycée in the city of his birth before coming to Paris in 1890 to study at the Ecole des Beaux-Arts. In 1895 he enrolled at the school in the studio of Gustave Moreau, where

*Henri Matisse*

he became the close friend and companion of another pupil, Henri Matisse. Marquet, one of the first of the Fauves, after 1898 painted landscapes at Arcueil and in the Luxembourg gardens, in strong, pure colors. From 1901, Marquet exhibited regularly at the Salon des Indépendants, later, at the Salon d'Automne, with Berthe Weill, and finally with the Druet Gallery, with which he signed a contract in 1905. He traveled all over Europe and North Africa painting the ever-changing scene of the great ports—Marseille, Le Havre, Naples, Hamburg, Rotterdam, Algiers, Istanbul, but he was probably happiest in Paris on the banks of the Seine. La Cité, Notre-Dame, the quays, and the Pont-Neuf fascinated him to the end.

*Bibliography:* G. Besson, *Marquet*, Crès, Paris, 1920; F. Fosca, *Albert Marquet*, Gallimard, Paris, 1922; G. Besson, *Marquet*, Crès, Paris, 1929; F. Jourdain, *Marquet*, Braun, Paris, 1948; L. Werth, *Eloge d'Albert Marquet*, Bruker, Paris, 1948; M. Marquet, *Marquet*, Laffont, Paris, 1951; F. Daulte and M. Marquet, *Marquet*, La Bibliothèque des Arts, Lausanne, 1953; F. Jourdain, *Albert Marquet*, Le Cercle d'Art, Paris, 1959; M. Sandoz, *Hommage à Marquet*, Bruker, Paris, 1963.

## HENRI MATISSE

Born December 31, 1869, at Cateau-Cambrésis (Nord); died November 3, 1954, at Cimiez (Alpes-Maritimes). Henri Matisse studied law and even worked for a solicitor for some time before turning to painting. In 1895 the young man joined the studio of Gustave Moreau, where he made friends with Marquet, Camoin, Henri Manguin and Georges Rouault. Four years later he attended life classes at the Academy Carrière and among the pupils met Jean Puy and André Derain, who soon introduced him to Maurice de Vlaminck. In company with his three new friends Matisse exhibited at the Salon des Indépendants of 1903 and two years later also participated in the Salon d'Automne in company with most of the other Fauves, who soon accepted him as their leader. During the winter of 1907–1908 Matisse opened an independent academy in the Convent of the Sacré-Cœur, where he taught many pupils, among them the German Hans Purrmann and the American Patrick Henry Bruce. Austere and restrained during his Cubist period, the painter became happy and relaxed after he had settled in the Midi in 1917. The art of Matisse flowered during the 1920s. Awarded the Carnegie Prize in 1927 Matisse went to the United States and painted the large decoration called *The Dance* for the Barnes Foundation at Merion, Pennsylvania, an important work which marked a turning point in his career. During the Second World War Matisse retired to Nice and finally Cimiez where he designed the plans and decoration for the Dominican chapel at Vence, and also devoted himself to tapestry, illustration, and collage.

*Bibliography:* M. Sembat, *Henri Matisse*, Gallimard, Paris, 1920; A. Basler, *Henri Matisse*, Junge Kunst, Leipzig, 1924; A. Barnes and V. de Mazia, *The Art of Henri Matisse*, Scribner, New York, 1933; R. Escholier, *Henri Matisse*, Floury, Paris, 1937; J. Cassou, *Matisse*, Braun, Paris, 1939; A. H. Barr, Jr., *Matisse, His Art and His Public*, The Museum of Modern Art, New York, 1951; A. Verdet, *Prestiges de Matisse*, Emile Paul, Paris, 1952; G. Diehl, *Matisse*, Tisné, Paris, 1954; J. Lassaigne, *Matisse*, Skira, Geneva, 1959; J. Leymarie, H. Read, and S. Liebermann, *Henri Matisse*, Chicago and Boston, 1966; J. Marchiori, *Matisse*, La Bibliothèque des Arts, Paris, 1967.

## HENRI MANGUIN

*Henri Manguin*

Born March 23, 1874, in Paris; died September 25, 1949, at Saint-Tropez. Like Marquet and Matisse, Henri Manguin enrolled in 1895 at the Ecole des Beaux-Arts and worked in the studio of Gustave Moreau. After 1902 Manguin exhibited in the Salon des Indépendants and from 1904 he hung in the Salon d'Automne paintings which could already be classed as Fauve for their intensity of color. In 1905 Manguin went to stay for a short time with Signac at Saint-Tropez and was so charmed by the little Provençal port that he bought a house there two years later. Henceforth only rare visits abroad—in particular a journey with Marquet to Naples in 1909—broke the peaceful existence of the artist. During the First World War the painter went to Switzerland where he stayed with the Hahnlosers at Winterthur and later at Colombier near Neuchâtel. Returning to France in 1920 Manguin fell into the habit of dividing his time between Paris, where he spent the winter, and his much-loved Provence where he stayed for the summer, especially at Saint-Tropez in the villa called "L'Oustalet." During the German occupation in 1940 Manguin rented a studio in the rue de la Banasterie at Avignon and subsequently stayed there for a few weeks every spring until he died.

*Raoul Dufy*

*Bibliography:* C. Terrasse, *Eloge d'Henri Manguin*, Bruker, Paris, 1954; E. Julien, *Préface de l'Exposition Manguin*, Musée d'Albi, Albi, 1957; P. Cabanne, *Manguin*, Ides et Calendes, Neuchâtel, 1964.

## RAOUL DUFY

Born June 3, 1877, at Le Havre; died March 23, 1953, at Forcalquier (Haute-Provence). After 1892 Raoul Dufy attended evening classes at the Ecole des Beaux-Arts in Le Havre. Othon Friesz was also a pupil and the two young men became friends. After his military service Dufy came to Paris in 1899 and joined the Bonnat studio in the Ecole des Beaux-Arts. He exhibited for the first time at the Salon des Indépendants in 1903 and in the Salon d'Automne of 1906. During that year he painted in the Fauve manner with Marquet at Sainte-Adresse near Le Havre and especially at Trouville. Two years later, working with Georges Braque at L'Estaque near Marseille, Dufy abandoned Fauvism under the short-lived influence of early Cubism. Later, in the course of many journeys to Provence and Italy, Dufy discovered the luminous atmosphere of the Midi. This new vision inspired him to paint in gouache and watercolor, and some great works resulted. In 1937 Dufy painted a monumental decorative mural entitled *La Fée Electricité* for the International Exhibition, which was a high point in his work. But at this time arthritis attacked the painter and troubled him until he died. In 1950 he went to Boston for treatment but unfortunately with little effect. Returning to France in 1952 Dufy settled at Forcalquier and while there had the joy of being awarded the Grand Prix of the Biennale at Venice.

*Bibliography:* P. Courthion, *Raoul Dufy*, Chroniques du Jour, Paris, 1928; C. Zervos, *Raoul Dufy*, Cahiers d'Art, Paris, 1928; M. Berr de Turique, *Raoul Dufy*, Floury, Paris, 1930; R. Jean, *Raoul Dufy*, Crès, Paris, 1931; P. Camo, *Dufy l'Enchanteur*, Marguerat, Lausanne, 1947; P. Courthion, *Raoul Dufy*, Cailler, Geneva, 1951; G. Besson, *Dufy*, Braun, Paris, 1953; A. Werner, *Dufy*, Abrams, New York, 1953; J. Lassaigne, *Dufy*, Skira, Geneva, 1954; F. Daulte, "Marquet et Dufy devant les Mêmes Sujets," *Connaissance des Arts*, Paris, November 1957.

## ANDRÉ DERAIN

Born June 10, 1880, at Chatou; died September 10, 1954, at Chambourcy (Seine-et-Oise). André Derain had already been painting for two years when he made friends with Vlaminck in 1900. Like Vlaminck, Derain painted landscapes at Chatou in pure watercolor and like him took part in the Salon d'Automne of 1905. But about 1907 Derain turned his back on Fauvism, discovered African Negro art, became excited by the work of Cézanne, and joined forces with Pablo Picasso and Amedeo Modigliani. After 1911 Derain adopted a more austere style—this was his so-called Gothic period—simplifying forms and using an almost monochrome palette. After the First World War Derain turned

*André Derain*

*Maurice de Vlaminck*

to classical art for inspiration, painting some portraits, powerful nudes, landscapes in the province of Var and at Saint-Maximin in the department of Lot, and skillfully composed still lifes. In 1935 Derain retired to Chambourcy to devote himself to his work as a theatrical designer, and to book illustration and sculpture, all of which was discovered only after his death.

*Bibliography:* D. Henry, *André Derain*, Klinkhardt und Biermann, Leipzig, 1920; E. Faure, *André Derain*, Crès, Paris, 1923; A. Salmon, *André Derain*, Gallimard, Paris, 1924; A. Basler, *Derain*, Albums d'Art, Druet, Paris, 1928; A. Salmon, *André Derain*, Chroniques du Jour, Paris, 1929; J. Leymarie, *André Derain ou le Retour à l'Ontologie*, Skira, Geneva, 1950; M. Sandoz, *Éloge de Derain*, M. Bruker, Paris, 1959; G. Hilaire, *André Derain*, Cailler, Geneva, 1959; D. Sutton, *A. Derain*, Phaidon, London, 1959; G. Diehl, *Derain*, Flammarion, Paris, 1964.

## MAURICE DE VLAMINCK

Born April 4, 1876, in Paris, died October 1, 1958, at La Tourillière (Eure-et-Loire). Vlaminck recounted several times the story of his youthful efforts to teach himself painting. Gifted with unusual physical strength, the young athlete of Chatou set off on a career as a professional cyclist and played the violin in small night clubs before turning his attention to painting. He took scarcely any lessons and developed from his own experience. In 1900 Vlaminck met Derain, and the two artists worked together at Chatou, today considered to be one of the cradles of Fauvism. The following year Derain introduced Vlaminck to Matisse as they came away, dazzled, from a Van Gogh exhibition at the Gallery Bernheim-Jeune. In 1905 Vlaminck exhibited for the first time at the Salon d'Automne and again in 1906 at Berthe Weill's. In that year Ambroise Vollard bought all the work in his studio. From 1908 to 1914 Vlaminck turned away from Van Gogh to follow in the steps of Cézanne in a more austere, solidly constructed style influenced by Cubism. After he became rich Vlaminck sought solitude and settled on a huge farm at La Tourillière, where he remained until his death, devoting his last years to landscape and still life and searching for the dramatic effects of chiaroscuro.

*Bibliography:* C. Coquiot, *Vlaminck*, L'Art et les Artistes, Paris, 1913; D. Henry, *Vlaminck*, Kahnweiler, Paris, 1913; F. Carco, *Vlaminck*, Gallimard, Paris, 1920; G. Duhamel, *Vlaminck*, Les Ecrivains Réunis, Paris, 1927; F. Fels, *Vlaminck*, Marcel Seheur, Paris, 1927; A. Mantaigne, *Vlaminck*, Crès, Paris, 1929; P. MacOrlan, *Vlaminck*, Le Chêne, Paris, 1945; M. Genevoix, *Vlaminck*, Flammarion, Paris, 1954; M. Sauvage, *Vlaminck, Sa Vie et Son Message*, Cailler, Geneva, 1956.

## ANDRÉ DUNOYER DE SEGONZAC

*André Dunoyer de Segonzac*

Born July 7, 1884, at Boussy-Saint-Antoine (Seine-et-Oise). After leaving the Lycée, Segonzac attended the lectures at the independent academy of Luc-Olivier Merson, then those given by Jean-Paul Laurens at the Julian Academy. While on military service Segonzac made friends with the painter Jean-Louis Boussingault and together they rented a studio at 37 rue Saint-André-des-Arts. The two friends spent the summer of 1908 at Saint-Tropez in company with Luc-Albert Moreau, in a villa rented from Signac, and there they painted their first landscapes. Called up in 1914 and posted to a camouflage unit, Segonzac sketched the *poilus*, sketches which he was to use as models for his etchings illustrating *Les Croix de Bois* by Roland Dorgelès. From 1920 to 1926 Segonzac spent all his time near Paris, particularly in the valley of the river Morin where he painted landscapes, nudes, and figures out of doors in a broad, rich manner. After 1926, though he never forgot the scenes of the Ile-de-France, his real home, he often spent the summer at Saint-Tropez, where he bought a third share with L.-A. Moreau and André Villebœuf in a house called "Le Maquis," close by "La Treille Muscate" owned by the writer Colette. Contact with the countryside of Provence and the practice of watercolor were responsible for the remarkable luminosity of his work. Apart from his oils and watercolors, Segonzac has achieved a remarkable position as an engraver. His etchings for Vergil's *Georgics* (1947) and for Ronsard's *Sonnets* (1955) rank among the masterpieces of modern engraving.

*Bibliography:* R. Jean, *A. Dunoyer de Segonzac*, Gallimard, Paris, 1922; J. Guenne, *A. Dunoyer de Segonzac*, M. Seheur, Paris, 1928; P. Jamot, *Dunoyer de Segonzac*, Floury, Paris, 1929; M. Gauthier, *Dunoyer de Segonzac*, Les Gémeaux, Paris, 1949; C. Roger-Marx, *Dunoyer de Segonzac*, Geneva, 1951; A. Liore and P. Cailler, *Catalogue de l'Œuvre Gravé de Dunoyer de Segonzac*, Vols. I to VI, Cailler, Geneva, 1951 ff.; B. Dorival, *Dunoyer de Segonzac*, Kister, Geneva, 1956; M.-P. Fouchet, *Dunoyer de Segonzac, Saint-Tropez et la Provence*, Paris, 1964.

*Georges Rouault*

## GEORGES ROUAULT

Born May 27, 1871, in Paris; died February 13, 1958, also in Paris. After an apprenticeship with a glass painter, Georges Rouault attended evening classes at the Ecole des Arts Décoratifs and in 1891 entered the Ecole des Beaux-Arts. There, like Matisse and Marquet, he was taught by Gustave Moreau, whose favourite pupil he became and who had a profound influence on him. However, Rouault failed in the competition for the Prix de Rome, although after the death of his teacher, he was made director of the Musée Gustave Moreau. From 1903 to 1908 Rouault regularly exhibited at the Salon d'Automne, of which he was one of the founding members. Influenced by the writer Léon Bloy, he painted, from 1902 to 1914, satirical compositions using prostitutes, clowns, and acrobats as models, canvases imbued with a vigor akin to Expressionism. Between 1914 and 1930 Rouault's style grew calmer and more varied. In turn landscapist and painter of Biblical subjects, the artist was also an engraver and illustrator. Among other things, he engraved the fifty-eight plates of the *Miserere* for Ambroise Vollard. During his last years Rouault concentrated on religious painting, and although he sometimes returned to his old themes—clowns or judges, for example—he always handled them in a serious, Christian style. In 1948 Rouault designed and produced stained-glass windows for the church at Assy.

*Bibliography:* M. Puy, *Rouault*, Gallimard, Paris, 1921; G. Charensol, *Georges Rouault*, Les Quatre Chemins, Paris, 1926; L. Venturi, *Georges Rouault*, Skira, Paris, 1948; J. Thrall Soby, *Georges Rouault, Paintings and Prints*, The Museum of Modern Art, New York, 1947; J. Maritain, *Georges Rouault*, Abrams, New York, 1952; B. Dorival, *Cinq Etudes sur Georges Rouault*, Editions Universitaires, Paris, 1956; B. Dorival, *Georges Rouault*, Kister, Geneva, 1956; S. Fukushima, *Georges Rouault*, Shinchosha, Tokyo, 1958; L. Venturi, *Rouault*, Skira, Geneva, 1959; P. Courthion, *Rouault*, Flammarion, Paris, 1962.

## PABLO PICASSO

Born October 25, 1881, at Malaga (Andalusia). After his first apprenticeship at Barcelona and Madrid, Picasso went to Paris in 1900. Influenced at first by Toulouse-Lautrec and Forain, he followed their example by painting genre scenes. Subsequently Picasso painted almost in monochrome—the "blue" (1901–1904) and "rose" (1905–1906) periods, when he painted blind beggars, lonely people, and harlequins. In 1906–1907 he discovered African Negro art and also came to a deeper appreciation and knowledge of the work of Cézanne. This experience resulted in 1907 in *Les Demoiselles d'Avignon*. Seeking ever more simplified forms, the painter joined forces with Juan Gris and Georges Braque, who were pursuing identical lines of research. Never satisfied, Picasso constantly sought to renew his inspiration. From 1911 to 1919 he developed from Analytical Cubism, which disintegrates form into small cubes and planes, to Synthetic Cubism, which, instead of reducing objects to their geometric lines, disperses these same lines to compose reality. About 1920,

*Pablo Picasso*

*Georges Braque*

after a journey to Italy, Picasso did a series of portraits with linear and austere features. However, he continued at the same time his researches into Synthetic Cubism, painting large still lifes and compositions such as *Les Trois Musiciens*. After 1929 Picasso turned once more to Expressionist art, the most typical examples of which are *Guernica*, a monumental composition inspired by the Spanish Civil War, and series of variations on a theme —for example those on Velásquez' *Meninas* and Delacroix's *Femmes d'Alger*.

*Bibliography:* A. Level, *Picasso*, Paris, 1928; B. Geiser, *Picasso, Peintre-Graveur (1899–1931)*, Geneva, 1931; F. Olivier, *Picasso et Ses Amis*, Stock, Paris, 1933; G. Stein, *Picasso*, Floury, Paris, 1938; A. Barr, *Picasso, Fifty Years of His Art*, The Museum of Modern Art, New York, 1946; A. Cirici-Pellicer, *Picasso avant Picasso*, Cailler, Geneva, 1950; M. Raynal, *Picasso*, Skira, Geneva, 1953; C. Zervos, *Pablo Picasso*, Catalogue, 10 Vols., Les Cahiers d'Art, Paris, 1932–1958; R. Cogniat, *Picasso–Figures*, La Bibliothèque des Arts, Paris; D.-D. Duncan, *Les Picassos de Picasso*, Edita, Lausanne – La Bibliothèque des Arts, Paris, 1961; P. Daix, G. Boudaille, and J. Rosselet, *Picasso 1900-1906*, Ides et Calendes, Neuchâtel, 1966.

## GEORGES BRAQUE

Born May 13, 1882, at Argenteuil; died August 31, 1963, in Paris. When his family settled at Le Havre in 1890 Georges Braque was eight years old. He was educated at the Lycée and subsequently studied at the Ecole des Beaux-Arts with Friesz and Dufy. At first he worked in the Impressionist style until 1906 when he assembled the Fauves and exhibited in the same year for the first time at the Salon des Indépendants. He painted with Friesz at Anvers in 1906, then at L'Estaque near Marseille with Dufy in 1907. Toward the end of 1907 Braque abandoned Fauvism in favor of a more austere, Constructivist style. He ranks with Picasso as one of the most important Cubist artists, evolving through Cubism's analytical and synthetic phases. Braque was severely wounded in 1915, underwent a trepanning operation, and did not paint again until 1917. For several years thereafter he was attracted by the idea of a return to classical painting. In 1924 Braque, for whom still life had almost always sufficed to express the universe around him, painted a series of large nudes, *Les Canéphores*. Three years later Braque bought a house at Varengeville near Dieppe, where he was to spend every summer, and there he started to paint landscapes of the Normandy beaches. Braque, who was also a decorator and sculptor, painted a ceiling for the Louvre (1952–53) and designed the cartoons for the stained glass in the chapel at Varengeville (1954–55).

*Bibliography:* F. Ponge, *Braque*, Skira, Geneva, 1946; A. Lejard, *Braque*, Hazan, Paris, 1949; J. Paulhan, *Braque le Patron*, Paris, 1952; M. Gieure, *Braque*, Tisné, Paris, 1956; J. Leymarie, *Braque*, Skira, Geneva, 1961; J. Richardson, *Braque*, La Bibliothèque des Arts, Paris, 1962; N. Mangin, *Catalogue de l'Œuvre de Georges Braque*, Maeght, Paris (in course of publication).

*Juan Gris*

## JUAN GRIS

Born March 23, 1887, in Madrid; died May 11, 1927, at Boulogne-sur-Seine. Although his parents intended him to become an engineer, Juan Gris (a pseudonym for José Gonzales) studied at the School of Arts and Crafts in Madrid, where he acquired a penchant for linear precision and clean construction. In 1906 Gris went to Paris, which he was never to leave again, and settled in the Bateau-Lavoir with his friend Picasso. To earn a living Gris contributed drawings for several years to satirical journals such as *Le Cri de Paris*, *L'Assiette au Beurre*, and *Charivari*. After 1910 he took part in the Cubist movement and was one of the pioneers of the technique of collage. During the war, after 1916, he painted still lifes and harlequins which may be said to be the outcome of Synthetic Cubism. When painting, the artist first composed a geometric plan on his canvas to give the work a fundamental frame, afterward adding ornament and partially destroying his geometry by using fragmentary images. "I turn a cylinder into a bottle," declared Gris. Apart from his work as a painter, Gris drew many illustrations and the programs for Diaghilev's Russian ballet and also designed sets for operas, notably Gounod's *La Colombe*.

*Bibliography:* M. Raynal, *Juan Gris*, L'Effort Moderne, Paris, 1920; D. Henry, *Juan Gris*, Klinkhardt und Biermann, Leipzig, 1929; W. George, Juan Gris, Gallimard, Paris, 1931; D.-H. Kahnweiler, *Juan Gris*, Gallimard, Paris, 1946; D. Cooper, *Juan Gris, ou le Goût du Solennel*, Skira, Geneva, 1959.

*Fernand Léger*

## FERNAND LÉGER

Born February 4, 1881, at Argentan in Normandy; died August 17, 1955, at Gif-sur-Yvette. Born of a line of Normandy peasants, Fernand Léger abandoned the land to follow his vocation. After an apprenticeship with an architect in Caen he came to Paris in 1903. Although he was not admitted to the Ecole des Beaux-Arts he was successful at the Ecole des Arts Décoratifs and afterward studied in Gerôme's studio and the Julian Academy. In 1908 Léger rented a studio in La Ruche, the community of artists in the Passage Dantzig, where he joined forces with Guillaume Apollinaire and Max Jacob. The dealer D.-H. Kahnweiler introduced him to Braque and Picasso in 1911, and he took part in the first Cubist exhibition in the Salon d'Automne. Léger, called up as a sapper in 1914, discovered the poetry of the machine, which he used as a predominant theme in his work after returning to civilian life (*Le Moteur*, 1918; *L'Homme à La Roue*, 1919; *La Ville*). The exhibition of decorative art held in 1925 gave him the chance to paint his first murals. At the same period Léger produced a film called *Le Ballet Mécanique*, which was to have considerable influence on the development of the cinema. Léger spent the years 1940–1945 in the United States, where he was given a warm welcome by American collectors and art lovers. After his return to France Léger enthusiastically took up new techniques—ceramics, polychrome sculpture, and tapestry. He made mosaics for the church at Assy (1946) and stained glass for Audincourt, Jura, in 1951.

*Bibliography:* M. Raynal, *Fernand Léger*, L'Effort Moderne, Paris, 1920; E. Teriade, *Fernand Léger*, Cahiers d'Art, Paris, 1928; F. Elgar, *Léger, Peintures 1911–1948*, Le Chêne, Paris, 1948; D. Cooper, *Fernand Léger et le Nouvel Espace*, Trois Collines, Geneva, 1949; P. Descargues, *Fernand Léger*, Le Cercle d'Art, Paris, 1955; R. L. Delevoy, *Léger*, Skira, Geneva, 1962; E. Tadini, *Léger, il Maestro di Colore*, Fabbri, Milan, 1964.

## ROGER DE LA FRESNAYE

Born July 11, 1885, at Le Mans; died November 27, 1925, at Grasse. Roger de La Fresnaye showed a remarkable talent for drawing while still very young. From 1908 he attended lectures by Maurice Denis and Serusier at the Ranson Academy. His contact with these men naturally made him an admirer of Cézanne and Gauguin. About 1911 he joined with the larger group of Cubists and took part in the exhibition called The Golden Section in company with Albert Gleizes, Jacques Villon, and Jean Metzinger. From 1912 to 1914 La Fresnaye painted works of great originality, combining abstract Cubism with the realism of independents such as Segonzac and Derain. An enthusiast for early aviation, La Fresnaye worked at this period for several months on a large composition called *La Conquête de l'Air*, his acknowledged masterpiece. Suffering from tuberculosis and the effects of gas during the First World War, La Fresnaye was evacuated to Tours in 1918. He retired to Hauteville and then to Grasse where he struggled for eight years against the

*Roger de La Fresnaye*

*Maurice Utrillo*

disease which killed him in his fortieth year. During this slow decline La Fresnaye gave up oil painting to devote all his force to drawing, color wash, and watercolor.

*Bibliography:* R. Allard, *Roger de la Fresnaye*, Paris, 1922; W. George, *Dessins et Gouaches de Roger de La Fresnaye*, Librairie de France, Paris, 1935; E. Nebelthau, *Roger de La Fresnaye*, Paul de Montaignac, Paris, 1935; R. Cogniat and W. George, *Œuvres Complètes de Roger de la Fresnaye*, Rivarol, Paris, 1950.

## MAURICE UTRILLO

Born December 26, 1883, in Paris; died November 5, 1955, at Dax (Landes). Maurice Utrillo, illegitimate son of Suzanne Valadon acknowledged by the critic Miguel Utrillo, attended the Rollin College before being apprenticed to a bank. Left to himself, he began to drink in secret and to lead the life of a tramp, until, at eighteen, after a severe attack, he had to undergo treatment for alcoholic poisoning. To amuse himself in his sick room his mother counseled him to draw. When he left the hospital, Utrillo began to paint his first pictures out of doors at Montmagny, Pierrefitte, La Butte-Pinson, Montmartre, and on the quays. Soon, however, Utrillo threw off the influence of Alfred Sisley and Camille Pissaro, and followed his pursuit of truth to the point of realism. During his "white period" (1909–1914), apart from a journey to Corsica and to Brittany, he painted Paris scenes, working from postcards in his studio. He was so intent on realism that he even went so far as to mix paste, sand, and plaster in pursuit of material effects. In 1926 Utrillo settled with his mother and André Utter in a new house in the Avenue Junot. All three went to Saint-Bernard (Ain) in summer, staying in a thirteenth-century chateau. At that time Utrillo's painting changed and this is now described as his "colored period," though it could as well be called "graphic," since clear colors and precise drawing are its chief characteristics. Shortly before the death of his mother, Utrillo in 1936 married Lucie Valore, with whom he spent his last years at Vésinet, near Chatou.

*Bibliography:* F. Carco, *Maurice Utrillo*, Gallimard, Paris, 1921; R. Rey, *Maurice Utrillo, Peintre et Lithographe*, Frapier, Paris, 1925; A. Tabarant, *Maurice Utrillo*, Bernheim-Jeune, Paris, 1926; F. Carco, *La Légende et la Vie d'Utrillo*, Grasset, Paris, 1928; G. Charensol, *Eglises et Cathédrales d'Utrillo*, Chroniques du Jour, Paris, 1929; A. Basler, *Maurice Utrillo*, Crès, Paris, 1931; P. Courthion, *Utrillo*, Marguerat, Lausanne, 1948; F. Jourdain, *Utrillo*, Paris, 1953; P. Pétridès, *L'Œuvre Complet de Maurice Utrillo*, Pétridès, Paris (in course of publication, Vols. I and II are already published); W. George, *Utrillo*, La Bibliothèque des Arts, Paris, 1960; R. Charmet, *Utrillo-Paris*, La Bibliothèque des Arts, Paris, 1963.

## JULES PASCIN

*Jules Pascin*

Born March 31, 1885, at Viddin in Bulgaria; died June 2, 1930, in Paris. Julius Pincas, called Jules Pascin, the son of a Spanish Jewish father and an Italian mother, lived in Vienna, Berlin, and Munich before settling in Paris in 1905. His regular contributions to the German periodical *Simplicissimus* had already made him famous, so that as soon as he arrived in Montparnasse the artist was welcomed with open arms by the artistic and cosmopolitan societies of the Dôme and Rotonde cafés. He contributed to several Parisian journals. In 1907 he became friends with Hermine David, a talented woman painter, whom he married ten years later. During the war Pascin, a Bulgarian, was forced to leave Paris and went to the United States where he became an American citizen. Although New York was his base, he traveled a great deal, returning with drawings and watercolors from Cuba, Texas, Florida, and South Carolina. In 1920 Pascin returned to Paris where he met Lucie

Krogh, wife of the Norwegian painter Per Krogh, and she became his mistress. At this period Pascin began to study engraving and sought advice from Jean-Gabriel Daragnès who taught him the craft. Poisoned by alcohol, divided in his affections, and a frequent visitor to brothels, where he filled many sketchbooks with voluptuous and nostalgic drawings, sometimes erotic but always imbued with inexpressible sadness, Pascin became unbalanced in mind. On the opening day of the exposition at the Georges Petit Gallery which was to bring him further success, the artist committed suicide.

*Bibliography:* G. Charensol, *Jules Pascin*, Le Triangle, Paris, 1928; I. Goll, *Pascin*, Crès, Paris, 1929; H. Brodsky, *Pascin*, Nicholson and Watson, London, 1946; A. Warnod, *Pascin*, Sauret, Monte Carlo, 1954; G. Papazoff, *Pascin ! Pascin ! C'est Moi !...*, Cailler, Geneva, 1959; A. Werner, *Pascin*, Abrams, New York, 1962.

*Marc Chagall*

## MARC CHAGALL

Born July 7, 1887, at Vitebsk in Russia. Son of a fairly poor Jewish family, Chagall was deeply influenced in childhood by the customs and traditions of his people. From 1907 to 1910 the young man attended the Imperial School of Fine Arts in St. Petersburg. There he met Léon Bakst, the decorator, who showed him the work of Cézanne and Gauguin and explained the import of the new movement in France. In 1910 Chagall went to Paris and stayed at La Ruche, the artists' colony, where Léger and Modigliani were already living. After an exhibition in 1914 in Berlin in the gallery run by the journal *Der Sturm*, Chagall went to Russia to marry his fiancée, Bella, the inspiration for many paintings of young lovers. Caught up by the war and the Revolution, Chagall was made Commissar of Fine Arts at Vitebsk and founded a school of eclectic painters. Returning to Paris in 1920 Chagall made the acquaintance of Ambroise Vollard, who asked him to do illustrations for Gogol's *Dead Souls*, La Fontaine's *Fables*, and the Bible. To prepare for the last, Chagall went to Israel in 1931. During the Second World War Chagall took refuge in the United States, where his reputation steadily increased. Among other things he designed the sets and costumes for Stravinsky's *Fire Bird*. In 1947 Chagall returned to France, dividing his time between Paris and Vence. During the last few years Chagall has done several large frescoes, notably the ceiling of the Opéra in Paris; he has also designed twelve stained-glass panels symbolizing the Tribes of Israel for the new medical center in Jerusalem.

*Bibliography:* A. Salmon, *Chagall*, Chronique du Jour, Paris, 1928; W. George, *Chagall*, Gallimard, Paris, 1928; R. Schwob, *Chagall et l'Ame Juive*, Corréa, Paris, 1931; R. Maritain, *Marc Chagall*, Edition de la Maison Française, New York, 1943; L. Venturi, *Marc Chagall*, New York, 1945; J. J. Sweeney, *Marc Chagall*, The Museum of Modern Art, New York, 1946; C. Estienne, *Chagall*, Somogy, Paris, 1951; G. Schmidt, *Chagall*, Hazan, Paris, 1952; L. Venturi, *Chagall*, Skira, Geneva, 1956; J. Lassaigne, *Chagall*, Maeght, Paris, 1957; F. Meyer, *Marc Chagall*, *L'Œuvre Gravé*, Calmann-Lévy, Paris, 1957; F. Meyer, *Marc Chagall*, Zurich, 1961.

## ANDRÉ PLANSON

Born April 10, 1898, at La Ferté-sous-Jouarre (Seine-et-Marne), not far from Château Thierry, the countryside of Corot and Couperin. Like his famous predecessors Planson closely links painting with music. After leaving the Lycée at Meaux the young man was taught by the landscape artist Paul Meslé who lived at Chamigny near La Ferté; then he went to Paris where, for a time, he attended courses at the Ranson Academy. However, it was in the valley of the Marne where he was born, rather than in Paris, that Planson's

*André Planson*

*Maurice Brianchon*

talent really developed. Although later the artist spent a long time in Brittany and Provence, he always returned to La Ferté, the place of his own choosing, where people and things were familiar. In 1933 Planson was awarded the Blumenthal Prize and from that date his painting was watched with interest by a growing circle of connoisseurs. The French nation also commissioned several important works. Among the most significant of these, the large mural decorations in the Lycée Janson-de-Sailly (1934) should be mentioned, also those for the theater of the Palais de Chaillot (1937), the Agricultural Institute of France and the Lycée at Enghien. Since the Second World War Planson has divided his time between Paris and the French countryside. At La Ferté, Le Pouldu, Villeneuve-lès-Avignon, and Vaison-la-Romaine, he pursues his task of landscape painter with zeal; in his studio in Paris he paints portraits, nudes, and scenes from the theater and ballet.

*Bibliography:* J. de Laprade, *André Planson*, Sequana, Paris, 1942; G. d'Assailly, *Avec les Peintres de la Réalité Poétique*, Julliard, Paris, 1949; P. MacOrlan, *André Planson*, Cailler, Geneva, 1954; A. Planson, *Carnet de la Marne* (introduction by A. Lanoux), La Bibliothèque des Arts, Paris, 1967.

## MAURICE BRIANCHON

Born January 11, 1899, at Fresnay-sur-Sarthe. After studying the classics at the Lycée of Le Mans and spending a short period at the Ecole des Beaux-Arts in Bordeaux, Maurice Brianchon joined the Ecole des Arts Décoratifs in Paris in 1917. There he attended the lectures of the brilliant and eclectic Eugène Morand, father of the future novelist, Paul Morand. In 1922 Brianchon left the Ecole des Arts Décoratifs and rented a studio in the Avenue du Maine, which he shared with his friend Raymond Legueult. At that time the two artists used to frequent the Medrano circus and the stage doors of the ballet and music halls. The award of the Blumenthal Prize in 1924 enabled Brianchon to travel to Spain. In Madrid he spent a long time in the Prado, studying Velásquez especially. After returning to France Brianchon scarcely left Paris, content to spend his summers on the Normandy or Brittany beaches he loved, particularly Trouville and Carnac. When he was thirty-five, Brianchon married on June 18, 1934, Marguerite Louppe, a painter with a very individual talent. Together they worked on three large mural paintings commissioned by the Conservatoire de Musique et d'Art Dramatique de Paris. During the years before the outbreak of the Second World War Brianchon did several decorative works: a large panel for the Lycée Janson-de-Sailly (1935) and two compositions for the Foyer de la Musique in the Palais de Chaillot (1936). Brianchon's activities as a theatrical designer should also be mentioned. For instance, he created the sets and costumes for *Les Fausses Confidences* by Marivaux, produced by Madeleine Renaud and Jean-Louis Barrault, and also for *La Seconde Surprise de l'Amour* by Marivaux. Since 1960 Brianchon has been working every summer in his country house, "Truffière," in Périgord.

*Bibliography:* R. Rey, *Maurice Brianchon*, Sequana, Paris, 1943; C. Roger-Marx, *Eloge de Brianchon*, Bruker, Paris, 1948; M. Zahar, *Maurice Brianchon*, Cailler, Geneva, 1949; G. d'Assailly, *Avec les Peintres de la Réalité Poétique*, Julliard, Paris, 1949; R. Heyd, *Brianchon*, Ides et Calendes, Neuchâtel, 1954; F. Daulte, *Catalogue de l'Exposition Brianchon*, Neuchâtel, 1962; M. Brianchon, *Carnet du Périgord* (introduction by F. Uhler), Ides et Calendes, Neuchâtel–La Bibliothèque des Arts, Paris, 1962.

## ROLAND OUDOT

*Roland Oudot*

Born July 23, 1897, in Paris. After studying in the Lycée Lavoisier Roland Oudot attended the same course as Brianchon and Legueult in the Ecole des Arts Décoratifs. After 1915 he worked with Léon Bakst, stage designer for the Russian ballet, then with Louis Süe and André Mare, interior designers. Roland Oudot's first landscapes represented the Ile-de-France. Later the artist worked in the Basque country, the Landes, Spain, and Italy. Successive exhibitions between 1924 and 1930, either as one of a group or alone, in the Portique Gallery, the gallery of Charles Auguste and the Valentine Gallery in New York gradually brought the work of Roland Oudot before the public. Collectors and such critics as Wilhelm Uhde and Louis Vauxcelles were impressed by the vigor and classical arrangement of his landscapes. They were attracted, too, by the mythological scenes and female figures, products of the very personal imagination of their creator. Apart from his easel pictures Roland Oudot did several mural paintings before 1940; for instance, he painted two panels for the entrance of the theater of the Palais de Chaillot, and the following year painted a large fresco on the theme "Grain" for the Agricultural Institute of Paris. During the years 1936, 1937, and 1938 Oudot discovered Provence and began to work near Saint-Rémy. After the Second World War the artist regularly went back and painted, in spring as in autumn, the view from his house at Eygallières, over the foothills of the Alps. In 1954 Roland Oudot bought the old manor of Vasouy near Honfleur, where he was to spend every summer painting the beaches and orchards of Normandy. Latterly Oudot has also stayed in Greece, New York, and especially Venice, where he has painted several masterpieces on the lagoon and at Chioggia.

*Bibliography:* C. Roger-Marx, *Roland Oudot, Drogues et Peintures*, Paris, 1937; P. Guégen, *Roland Oudot*, Sequana, Paris, 1942; G. d'Assailly, *Avec les Peintres de la Réalité Poétique*, Julliard, Paris, 1949; C. Roger-Marx, *Roland Oudot*, Cailler, Geneva, 1952; C. Roger-Marx, *Eloge de Roland Oudot*, Bruker, Paris, 1958; F. Daulte, *Catalogue de l'Exposition Oudot*, Neuchâtel, 1963; R. Oudot, *Carnet de Provence* (introduction by P. Cabanne), La Bibliothèque des Arts, Paris, 1963; D. Vouga, *Roland Oudot*, Flammarion, Paris, 1964.

*Raymond Legueult*

## RAYMOND LEGUEULT

Born in Paris May 10, 1898 Raymond Legueult entered the Ecole des Arts Décoratifs in 1914 and worked under the supervision of an enthusiastic and eclectic master, Eugène Morand. In that studio the young man met two other pupils, Roland Oudot and Maurice Brianchon, who became his friends. In 1923 Legueult received a traveling scholarship which enabled him to visit Spain and to copy some of the paintings by Velásquez and El Greco in the Prado. Shortly after his return he was made a professor at the age of twenty-six in the Ecole des Arts Décoratifs. At that time he was living in a studio in the Avenue du Maine which he shared with Brianchon. For several years the two artists painted side by side, decorating together the sets for *Grisélidis* (1925) at the Paris Opéra and for *La Naissance de la Lyre* (1928). In 1937 Legueult painted a large decoration for the Salle d'Honneur in the Collège des Jeunes Filles at Fontainebleau. His panel, representing *Spring*, shows a procession of dancers executing a *farandole*. At this period the artist moved to the rue Boissonade. He still lives there today and in the quiet of his studio paints, in a subtle, colored style figures, still lifes, and large landscapes sketched on the beach of Porquerolles or in the garden of "Les Sorbiers." In 1956 Legueult was made professor and head of the painting studio in the Ecole Nationale des Beaux-Arts of Paris and four years later a whole room was devoted to his work at the Venice Biennale.

*Bibliography:* R. Jean, *Raymond Legueult*, Sequana, Paris, 1943; G. d'Assailly, *Avec les Peintres de la Réalité Poétique*, Julliard, Paris, 1949; M. Zahar, *Legueult*, Flammarion, Paris, 1962.

## YVES BRAYER

*Yves Brayer*

Born November 18, 1907, at Versailles. After attending the Lycée at Bourges Yves Brayer worked in the academies of Montparnasse before going, in 1926, to the Ecole des Beaux-Arts in Paris. In 1927 a state traveling scholarship enabled the young man to go to Spain and to visit Madrid, and the Escorial, Toledo, and Granada. Spain and its painters had great influence on Brayer in the years to come. Awarded the Grand Prix de Rome in 1930 he went to Italy, remaining a long time, and returned home with many townscapes, gouaches and monotypes of Roman life and scenes in the Vatican. Two years later, in 1932, Brayer went to Greece and Istanbul. The outbreak of war in 1939 found the artist in London where he had been working for several months and he returned to France to join the army. Demobilized at Montauban in 1940, Yves Brayer settled at Cordes (Tarn) as he was attracted by the colorful buildings of Albi and its surroundings. In 1941, however, Jacques Rouché sought him out to do the designs and costumes for two ballets at the Opéra: *Joan de Zarissa* and *L'Amour Sorcier*. Brayer found a new source of inspiration in the ballet and theatrical world. A painter of the Mediterranean, after 1943 the artist developed the habit of going regularly to work in Provence. Abandoning architecture, he turned to pure landscape and his canvases of the foothills of the Alps and of the lakes of the Camargue mark a new stage in his development. He went to Mexico in 1964 and brought home a richly colored series of watercolors. Recently he visited Cairo and Upper Egypt. Brayer has, in the course of his career, executed large mural paintings for steamships and for public buildings, notably the Post Office in the rue de la Boëtie in Paris, the prefectures at Nimes and Nevers, and the technical college of Bourges.

*Bibliography:* P. du Colombier, *Yves Brayer*, Melot, Paris, 1944; M. Gauthier, *Yves Brayer*, Les Gémeaux, Paris, 1948; A. Chamson, *Yves Brayer*, Cailler, Geneva, 1958; J. Bouret, *Eloge d'Yves Brayer*, Bruker, Paris, 1955; Y. Brayer, *Carnet du Maroc* (introduction by J. Giono), La Bibliothèque des Arts, Paris, 1963; Y. Brayer, *Carnet de Camargue* (introduction by P. Cabanne), La Bibliothèque des Arts, Paris, 1965; J. Giono, *Yves Brayer*, La Bibliothèque des Arts, Paris, 1966.

## GEORGES ROHNER

*Georges Rohner*

Born July 20, 1913, in Paris. After leaving secondary school Georges Rohner attended the Ecole des Beaux-Arts, where he made the acquaintance of Humblot, and in company with other friends, notably Francis Gruber and Jannot, they formed a group called significantly New Forces. Admirers of La Fresnaye, Rohner and his friends attempted to reintroduce a sense of order and a taste for construction into painting. Before the Second World War, Rohner exhibited almost exclusively at the Carmine Gallery and the Salon des Indépendants. Called up in 1939, he was taken prisoner in the Vosges and did not return to France until three years later. After the war he showed his canvases at the Barreiro Gallery, then at Framond, and finally, since 1965, at the Galerie de Paris. An objective painter, Rohner has succeeded in giving his still lifes and figures a poetic and highly individual atmosphere. Like Despierre and Roland Oudot, Rohner has also played an important role in the renaissance of tapestry, by designing many cartoons for the Manufacture Nationale des Gobelins and for Aubusson. He also composed important mosaics and mural paintings for the Lycées of Bourges, Orly, Annecy, Brest, and Annonay. The years 1965 and 1966 Rohner spent in Rome. Excited by the architecture of the Eternal City, its squares, fountains, museums, and gardens he brought home many drawings and watercolors, which have enabled him to finish in his studio several large canvases which rank among the masterpieces of modern painting.

*Bibliography:* R. Rey, *Georges Rohner*, Flammarion, Paris, 1957; P. Cabanne, *Rohner, Peintures*, Galerie de Paris, Paris, 1965; G. Rohner, *Carnet de Rome* (introduction by P. du Colombier), La Bibliothèque des Arts, Paris, 1966.

## MICHEL CIRY

*Michel Ciry*

Born August 31, 1919, at La Baule (Loire-Inférieure). While still a student in Paris Michel Ciry was already drawing and engraving in 1935. In 1938 he was invited to contribute to an exhibition entitled Artists of Our Time, where, for the first time he showed an important group of his graphic works. After this first appearance Ciry became recognized as a painter of solemn, austere subjects. For many years, until about 1952, the artist devoted himself almost entirely to engraving, drawing, and illustration, and apart from several attempts with oils in 1942 and 1943, which he repudiated and subsequently destroyed, it was not until the autumn of 1952 that Michel Ciry started to paint again in a continuous way. Without laying aside his engraving altogether—he has already completed nearly four hundred plates—the artist now gave nearly all his attention to painting. Since 1960 he has also been drawn to watercolor, a technique in which he was immediately successful. After working for many years at Chatou in the Ile-de-France, Michel Ciry moved in 1965 to an old farm at Varengeville where he found his inspiration in the orchards and beaches of Normandy. Apart from his French landscapes and others done on journeys to Venice, Toledo, Orvieto, New York, and Montreal, Ciry holds an important position as a figure painter. A perceptive portraitist and draftsman with a gift for analysis of the human face, Michel Ciry is not daunted by large compositions. His *Saul, Hommages to Bernanos*, and series of *Harlequins* and *Pierrots*, exhibited in 1964 and 1966 at the Galerie de Paris, prove how well he has solved the problems presented by large surfaces.

*Bibliography:* N. Bettex-Cailler, *Michel Ciry*, Art-Document, Geneva, 1957; M. Ciry, *Carnet de Venise* (introduction by G. Bauer), La Bibliothèque des Arts, Paris, 1963; M. Ciry, *Carnet d'Assise* (introduction by F. Fosca), La Bibliothèque des Arts, Paris, 1964; P. Mazars, *Michel Ciry*, Cailler, Geneva, 1966; F. Daulte, *Michel Ciry*, La Bibliothèque des Arts, Paris, 1966; R. Passeron, *L'Œuvre Gravé de Michel Ciry (1949-1954),* La Bibliothèque des Arts, Paris, 1968.

The photographs reproduced in this book are from the author's records.


This book was printed and bound
by Imprimerie Paul Attinger S. A., Neuchâtel.
The photolithos of the color plates are by Atesa, Geneva.
Layout by André Rosselet, Auvernier (Switzerland).


Printed in Switzerland.